Lessons From A Cult Survivor

By Claire Ashman

ABOUT THE AUTHOR

On 16th August 2006 Claire Ashman walked away from 30 years of strict religious indoctrination and a lifetime spent in a sect and a cult. She had overcome seemingly insurmountable odds to achieve this freedom for the first time in her life.

Claire set about creating a new life for herself and her 8 children, educating herself any way she could. This led to Claire giving 4 TEDx talks in the space of 2 years as well as numerous TV interviews.

It's is Claire's desire to broaden understanding and create open dialogue surrounding New Religious Movements (NRMs), Sects and Cults; especially for those who leave these groups and are forging new lives in the world.

You can find Claire at:

www.ClaireAshman.com

IngramSpark

First published 2018 by Ingram Spark

Copyright © 2018 Claire Ashman.

All rights reserved. Except as permitted under the *Australian Copyright Act 1968*, no part of this publication may be reproduced, stored in a retrieval system, or transmitted in any form or by any means, electronic, mechanical, photocopying, recording or otherwise, without prior written permission from the publisher. All enquiries should be made to the author.

 A catalogue record for this book is available from the National Library of Australia

978-0-6482634-0-1 (paperback)

Cover design by Kathryn Eggins
Edited by Mary Gebhart Editorial Services
Typeset in 10 pt Times New Roman

Disclaimer

Some names have been altered to keep the identities of some individuals private.

ACKNOWLDEGEMENTS

This book is dedicated to my beautiful children who walked this journey with me - my love for you all propelled me to do my utmost to provide a better life for you all. You all have a very special piece of my heart. I am proud of each and every one of you.

My dear husband Mark - although you landed on the scene much later your loving support, belief and encouragement means the world to me. Thank you for coming into my life and bringing me love, joy, humour and romance.

Much love and appreciation to Kay, Arnie, Nathaniel, Jessica.

Mary and Dale – your unwavering support, friendship and love through the years has meant the world to me.

Mary Gebhart who did an amazing job of editing this book.

Chapter 1 – Friday

In early August 2006, it was a cold, but sunny winter day in Nowra. I was going about my usual daily routine which included doing housework and looking after my children whilst my husband Tony sat in front of the computer in the office he'd built pretending to work whilst in reality he was gambling away time, money and our lives.

Outside the window, I could see a car slowly climbing the steep driveway. As it came into view, I could see it was a police car and I wracked my brain to think what on earth we had done to warrant a visit from the authorities. As residents of William Kamm's Order of St. Charbel, we'd become familiar with the local police as they'd investigated Kamm for a variety of violations, but I was at a loss as to what anyone in our family could have done to spark such a visit.

I put on a cheerful smile and went to greet them because I'd always believed that a happy manner often turned around a potentially difficult situation and because I'd been raised to be a "nice girl." I called to Tony to come join me, but he didn't respond.

I wasn't surprised. Our marriage had been going south for a long while, and Tony had spent the best part of the previous two years ignoring me. I squared my shoulders and prepared to deal with the police officers the same way I'd dealt with many of the difficult things that had come my way during my marriage -- alone.

I opened the door and cheerily greeted both the officers.

John introduced himself and his partner, and then went on to explain that they were there to serve Tony and I with mortgage repossession papers. I didn't understand what that meant so I asked him to please explain. Tony had not yet appeared, so John handed me the papers whilst he told me that Kamm had not paid the mortgage for quite some time and, as a result, the house we were living in was being repossessed.

"What does that mean?" I asked as I looked up from the papers I didn't understand.

"I'm sorry, ma'am, but it means that you have twelve days to find somewhere else to live," he replied with an apologetic half smile.

I could not believe my ears! I'd wanted out of the St. Charbel compound from the moment we'd arrived in 1997, and for the past two years, I'd been actively looking for opportunities to leave, but I certainly had never expected to be *evicted*!

As John continued to explain the procedure, I felt a little bit of excitement well up inside me.

Wait till the kids came home from school and I tell them! I thought to myself. *They're going to be over the moon!*

I tried to bring my attention back to focus on what the Sheriff was saying as he told me that I needed to find a house to rent and that if I trouble finding one before the twelve days were up, then I should call the housing commission and they would help me.

"My children and I have wanted to move from here for so long, you've now given us this wonderful opportunity," I said excitedly. "Thank you *so* much! We won't give you any trouble at all."

John seemed more than a little surprised by my enthusiastic response to being evicted from my home, but he smiled and, again, told me that I should contact the housing commission if I had any problems.

After the officers left, I took the papers in to Tony, who was still sitting and staring at his computer screen.

"We're being evicted," I bluntly told him. "We have twelve days to move."

Tony's expression didn't change nor did he say anything. He simply pushed the papers aside and continued gambling. I stood next to his desk waiting to see if he would speak, and when he didn't, I walked out.

I thought to myself, *I don't care one iota what he thinks or feels, the kids and I are going to take this chance to move, no matter what!*

My mind was swimming with hundreds of thoughts and, as a result, I didn't know what to do first. I'd never applied for a rental by myself before, and I had no idea how to go about it. In an effort to calm my nerves, I decided to do the practical thing and begin cleaning.

When the kids arrived home later that afternoon, I teased them with, "Guess who visited us today?!" They had no clue, and as I filled them in on the Sheriff's visit huge smiles spread across their faces and they excitedly began high-fiving each other --and me.

"Mum, go to the school and explain everything to them! They will give us the week off and we will organize everything at home and look after the younger kids," my three older assured me. "You just go get a pile of boxes and look for houses."

As good as it felt to have the support of my teenage children, it also served as a depressing reminder that my husband was not, nor would he ever be, excited about moving out of the compound or supportive of my desire to do so.

Later that night, I rang Scottie, Tony's employer, and told him the day's events. He was excited for me and knowing that Tony wouldn't cope well with this news, told me to send Tony down in Goulburn on Monday and if he questioned why, tell him that Scottie said he was needed.

Excellent, I thought. *The kids and I will be free to organize the move.*

My mind was still buzzing when I went to bed, but I was excited that my kids and I now had a way out of this horrible cult.

Chapter 2 – Back to the Beginning

People often ask me how someone like me could end up in a cult. The reality is that around the world tens of thousands of people follow charismatic leaders and belong to groups that can be classified as cults. Some people choose to follow and others, like myself, join because we are tethered to the underlying beliefs even when we have serious misgivings about those teaching them. What's important to understand is that I wound up in a cult for a variety of reasons, and in order to understand how I arrived here, I need to go back and explain where I came from.

My parents were both raised as Catholics, though neither of them was particularly devout nor were their families.

They attended mass on Sundays and celebrated the Catholic

holidays, but beyond that no one in either family recalls anything particularly extreme about Mum or Dad when they were growing up.

Dad's mum, my beloved Nanna, told us that in her younger days she couldn't make up her mind about whether she wanted to be a nun or wait for the right man and get married, so she made plans to "try out" convent life for a month hoping it would make things clearer. A few weeks before she entered the convent, she met Grandad and went out on a few dates with him. Nanna knew there was something special about Grandad, but since she'd already committed to spending a month in the convent, off she went and spent the entire month thinking about Grandad. At the end of the month, she returned home and asked Grandad to be her partner for a dance at the local hall. When he responded, "Would you be my partner for life?" she knew she'd made the right decision leaving the convent behind.

Dad was born in 1939 in Central Victoria and was the eldest of five children (one of whom died soon after birth).

Although he was a bright student and scored high enough on standardized exams to place in the top five for Mathematics in the state, he was forced to leave school early to help my grandfather manage and maintain the family farm. In the early 1950's, according to my grandfather, it was more important that his eldest son help support the family than be clever at school. Despite the break in his studies, Dad became a pig judge and wool classer, and then secretly studied to become an accountant while helping Grandad run the farm.

It wasn't until decades later that I learned dad had covertly applied for accountant jobs. He'd not only loved Maths but had also wanted to create a much better life for himself and his future family. When his strict paternal grandmother found out that Dad was still going to school, she tore shreds off him by scolding, "How dare you try to better yourself? Your job is to help your father run the farm, so your brothers can attend boarding school!" Since Dad was sensitive and had respect for his elders, he promptly ditched any further ideas of being an accountant and continued helping Grandad on the farm.

Mum's upbringing was different from Dad's. The eldest of three daughters, she grew up near Colac in western Victoria in a family heavily influenced and run by women. My grandfather left the family when Mum was only three years old and when my grandmother was unable to support the girls without a husband, she went to live with her mother bringing her little daughters with her. When I was young, Mum almost never talked about her lack of a father, but years later I'd come to understand that she felt deeply ashamed about it.

Mum had two younger sisters, Marie and Monica, and their mother (my Mama) was extremely strict. She was a firm believer in "spare the rod, spoil the child" and her rod of choice was a large wooden spoon. Mama's husband abandoned the family not long after

Monica was born, and Mum always felt a deep shame about being fatherless.

Monica, the youngest sister, was a prominent figure in our lives. We didn't see her often as she was busy with her own, seemingly glamorous single life in Melbourne, working and traveling for an implant company. When she did visit, there was great excitement; especially for my sisters and I. Monica was the epitome of fashion that we never experienced. Her hair and make-up were always impeccable, and she seemed so ladylike and stylish. We admired her from afar and longed to emulate her elegance.

My sisters and I loved it when Monica gave us her excess makeup. We had no idea how to apply it properly, but it was great fun experimenting. Whenever Mum caught us playing with the gifted makeup, she was very disapproving. She'd mutter that we were "spoiling God's beauty" and had "no need of that awful stuff on your face." Mum didn't talk about Auntie Monica much, and when she did it was to lament that Monica lived "life of sin and not only enjoyed it but showed no remorse for her wrongdoing." Often when talking to Mama on the phone, Mum would drag the phone into the other room and have whispered conversations about whatever naughty things Monica seemed to be up to.

All I knew was that whatever Auntie Monica was up to, she was definitely happier than mum was.

Mum's other sister, Marie, was an enigma. After completing high school Marie joined the now extinct Blessed Sacrament Sisters who had one of their convents in the Melbourne suburb of Malvern. I had seen the photo Dad and Mum had taken with her on their wedding day, which had been snapped inside the convent before Marie was due to take her final vows. It was shortly after this that she was told by her superiors that she didn't have a vocation and was asked to leave. Marie never quite explained why she was asked to leave nor did she ever accept the decision. Years later Nanna told me that Marie had trouble being obedient and as this is a definite prerequisite for convent life, she obviously didn't fit in. For a short while she worked in a plant nursery then studied to become a Childhood Community Nurse and loved telling the story about how she was working in the Echuca hospital when my brother Matthew was born in 1972.

Marie had been born with eye problems that no doctor had diagnosed correctly or ever treated effectively. Her sight problems grew worse as she grew older, and she had several operations over the years to try and fix the problem, but they had failed. As a result, she was prone to accidents, often hurting her knees when she'd trip and fall. The constant falls badly damaged her knees and caused her constant pain, and in seeking relief from the pain, Marie became addicted to very strong painkillers.

Dad was not a fan of Marie's, in fact, he actively disliked her and never tried to hide it. In 1982, Marie came to stay with us after she slipped in the church hall in Hampton and hurt her knee. A doctor friend prescribed her a sleeping drug and unfortunately hadn't asked all the appropriate questions before prescribing. That first night Marie assured mum that she needed 2 tablets in order to sleep properly but when morning came, and she didn't stir, it was a cause for grave anxiety. Mum freaked out because she had been the one to allow Marie to take the higher dosage and being a nurse, she should have known better.

It was quite the drama because at that point that the ambulance and police arrived, Marie's problem was seen as a drug overdose and no one knew that she had actually suffered a stroke. Marie was initially taken to Ballarat Hospital, then later transferred to another hospital in Melbourne. Mum was very stressed, not knowing how bad the stroke was nor the damage done. Astonishingly enough Marie awoke almost unscathed, then came back to our house to recover. Over the next few months mum had to teach her the basics all over again, how to walk, assisting her toileting, showering, dressing and eating. It was then decided to build her a little "convent," just up the hill from our house so that mum could keep an eye on her. Again, dad did not like the close proximity of her living there, but went ahead with building a small one bedroom flat with a kitchenette and shortly after she moved in.

After she'd moved into her little house, I used to visit Auntie Marie quite a bit just to talk because she seemed really lonely and, quite frankly, so was I. Our priest, Fr. Cummins, bought her an altar bread making machine and I used to help her make the communion wafers that Fr. Cummins would consecrate for mass. Performing this needed service gave her a small sense of purpose.

It was during one of these visits that Auntie Marie let slip the secret about Mum's time in the convent. I was sixteen at the time, and this came as a massive surprise, yet it also explained why mum had been very cagey about her life whenever we'd asked questions. Dad on the other hand was always quite open about his life and often had very funny stories to tell about the antics he got up to. My siblings and I had often questioned mum about a lovely photo she had on her dresser, of her and a very handsome young man on the night she made her debut. We were curious about whether they were ever a couple or not and also if there had been any other boyfriends on the scene before dad. Mum always evaded answering our questions or changed the subject and we'd always wondered why. It seemed odd to us that she'd completed her schooling, celebrated by making her debut then studied nursing in Western Australia, and that she'd never owned a car before meeting dad or gone out with any other guys. This revelation about her time in the convent now made complete sense, but I couldn't figure out why on earth she'd kept it a secret.

By the time I got home from Auntie Marie's Mum had already left for work, so as soon as Dad walked in the door I announced,

"Mum was in the convent."

"She bloody well wasn't," Dad hotly denied. I could tell something was up because he stiffened as he said this.

"Yes, she did because Auntie Marie told me so," I shot back.

Dad was angry that Auntie Marie had let the cat out of the bag, but I couldn't understand why it bothered him so much. I cornered mum the next day and told her I knew about her being a nun.

"So?" she answered in an off handed manner.

"But why didn't you tell us? When we asked you all those questions about whether you ever went out with other guys or why you didn't own a car, why didn't you explain to us you were in the convent?" I insisted.

Mum replied that she didn't consider it a big deal. But I did. I felt there had to have been a reason for her hiding her past, and if there wasn't, then it made no sense why she'd continue to refuse to talk about it.

I waited until we next visited Nanna, our father's mother, and I told her about what I'd learned.

"Yes, your mother told your father on their very first date," Nanna replied calmly. "When he came home after that date the first words out of his mouth were, "She spent time in the bloody convent!" He felt embarrassed that she'd been a nun before they met."

What I finally discovered was that Mum had left for the St. John of God nursing convent in Subiaco, Western Australia, straight after finishing school. For the first few years everything went well, but then Mum became covered in psoriasis. At the time, this was considered a Sign from God that she hadn't been called to the life and didn't have a vocation. She was given various medications to see if the psoriasis would disappear, but nothing helped and when her diseased skin wasn't healed, her superiors that decided that she should leave religious life. Mum had no say in the decision and afterward she returned to Victoria to live with my grandmother and completed her nursing degree in Melbourne.

Mum and Dad dated for a while, and Dad would fondly recall the days when Mum would wear a crocheted white bikini while sun baking in the front yard. They were married in a Catholic Church in Malvern, Melbourne in 1969 with Mum wearing a dress she'd made herself.

Initially they lived in Echuca since that's where dad was still working on Grandad's farm. Mum was working at the hospital before she had me in 1970 and returned there after I was born. Shortly after my brother Matthew was born, in 1972, my parents made the decision to move three hours south to Ballarat because they wanted a fresh start. Mum went back to work at the hospital whilst dad worked at a caravan company, installing the innards. Dad and Mum bought a house in the Ballarat suburb of Wendouree in 1973 and shortly afterwards, my twin siblings, Marisha and

Dominic, were born. When they were about a year old, mum returned to night shifts whilst dad looked after us.

Looking back on that time, I can remember crouching on the carpet in the hall doorway, watching Dad mop the kitchen floor while my siblings slept in the bedrooms nearby.

Mum deemed extended family not good company for us to mix with due to the differences in Catholic outlook; however, we did visit both grandmothers quite often. My maternal grandmother lived quite close, and she was a housekeeper for a Catholic priest in a small town about 40 minutes away. We did like getting out of the house and going to Mama's meant we would be spoilt on good food and dessert (the latter a rare treat in our house). For my sisters and I, it also provided the opportunity to secretly take a magazine out of the huge pile, find a quiet corner and settle down to read the gossip of the world while trying to make sure Mum didn't catch us. It didn't always happen though, since Mum kept an eagle eye on those magazines – and us.

After we had our fill of good food, my siblings and I would happily wander around the adjoining properties and fields, exploring and picking wild flowers. It was rare that Dad came with us for a visit to Mama because he didn't like her much, and when he would visit, his behaviour made us anxious as he often got quite annoyed and would take off in the car in a temper, leaving us all behind. He'd show up a few hours later, hurrying us into the car so we could go home. Sometimes he was still so angry that he'd erupt in road rage on the way home, too. We had no idea what caused these outbursts, so we sat silent and nervous in the back of the car hoping that there wouldn't be an accident.

Nanna, our father's mother and our favourite grandmother, lived three hours away in Echuca, so we didn't visit her as often. We loved visiting Nanna because she was *always* genuinely interested in all that we did.

"How are the little people?" she would ask, scurrying off to make tea for the "big people" as she called adults.

"The Big People can get a bit grumpy", she'd whisper to us. "So, let me make them a cuppa and biscuits, then I'll hear your news."

We'd patiently wait till the adults were served, then Nanna would listen to us chatter about everything, asking questions as she scurried about the kitchen. It was always comforting to visit Nanna and hear stories of her childhood as we watched her peel potatoes that later she would mash into fluffy clouds of white deliciousness that melted in your mouth. After Nanna filled our tummies, we'd go exploring in the cupboard under the stairs for the charity store treasures that Nanna would find for us during her volunteer hours. If the adults were distracted in conversation, we would tiptoe up the polished stairs to find more treasures upstairs.

My favorite treasure was Nanna's wedding dress. A very simple, slimming elegantly designed garment that we were allowed to carefully dress up in, as long as we put it back. Once we finished our inside explorations, we'd play hide and seek in Nanna's well-tended garden. During the spring and early summer months, we ventured outside the front gate to eat our fill of delicious, red squishy overripe plums from the trees that lined Nanna's street. One of our cousins was amazed that we could eat so many and not get sick!

Nanna was very devoted to Granddad, who died of cancer when I was eight. Even though I was quite young, I remember visiting him before he went to hospital and Nanna tenderly looking after him before he died.

Although we didn't see Nanna as often, her influence on us all, particularly myself, was very strong. She was constantly passing on valuable little life lessons and wise sayings that I still live by. Nanna was loved by all who knew her because she genuinely took an interest in everyone and their family.

Locals knew that Mary McAuliffe would always welcome a visit and listen with patience and kindness to your troubles.

Whenever someone asked her how she was she invariably replied, "There is always someone worse off than yourself in the world."

#

As Catholics we attended Mass every Sunday in the church a few kilometres away, and sometimes on other special Holy Days. This little church was on the edge of seminary grounds, it had been the training ground for Redemptorist priests. The intricate beauty of this old building and the colourful stained glass windows never failed to leave me awed, and Mum taught us to tiptoe into church so our shoes wouldn't make a sound on the cold marble floor as we made our way to our pew. I was so distracted by the large red glowing sanctuary lamp and the wafting of incense that signified Jesus was living in the tabernacle, that I'd often forget to genuflect to show my respect to Him there, and, as a four-year-old, Mass always seemed very long and boring to me, but when the organist would play the deep, rich sound of the pipe organ never failed to catch and hold my attention.

This Congregation of the Most Holy Redeemer (C.Ss.R.), a community of Roman Catholic priests and lay brothers, had been founded by St. Alfonso Maria de'Liguori at Scala, Italy, in 1732 and made its way to Australia in the late 19th Century. The Redemptorists were devoted to Our Lady of Perpetual Help (the Virgin Mary) and were tasked with the job of ministering to the poor and sharing God's message with those in most need of spiritual guidance. Throughout the first half of the 20th century, Redemptorist communities flourished as priests were sent out around the globe to minister to those in need by promoting social justice.

In the latter half of the 20th century, things began to change within the Catholic Church and between 1962 and 1965 the Second Vatican Council wrestled with how to align the Catholic Church with modern society. The debates would take place under the watchful eye of two Popes (Pope John XXIII and Pope Paul VI), and would lead to changes (such as allowing mass to be celebrated in the language of the community, eliminating the extravagant vestments that the priests wore during Mass, and allowing the priest to face the congregation instead of facing the altar) that not only caused a schism in the Church itself, but would also deeply affect the lives of Catholic families like mine.

It was whilst attending Mass here that my parents befriended Fr. Cummins, an elderly priest who preferred to adhere to the old methods of Catholicism by saying Mass in the pre-1962 manner. This was known as the Tridentine Mass and unlike the post-Vatican II Mass, which was performed in the language of the community in which it was being celebrated, the Tridentine Mass was celebrated solely in Latin.

Fr. Cummins wore a long, black cassock that had big rosary beads hanging from the waist and used all the old Roman vestments when he said Mass. It wasn't long after Mum befriended him that life changed dramatically in our house.

While our family had been considered "good Catholics" (attending Mass in our local parish on Sundays and holy days and saying a few prayers at home), all of a sudden, worship was taken to a whole new level.

Fr. Cummins started saying the Latin Mass privately in our

lounge room at Wendouree. At first, it was just our family, but before long there were more people coming every time.

Mum insisted on more prayers being said, outside influences were slowly eliminated (the television wasn't replaced when it blew up) and altogether, we seemed to become more religiously devout. A couple of times when I got up at night, Mum and Dad would be chanting litanies of prayers before their bedtime. I was young and didn't understand this new fascination with prayer, but I knew for certain that I didn't like the new boundaries being drawn around my freedom.

The real turning point came one day when Mum interrupted my play and told me I had to change my clothes because we were going to visit a priest. Despite the fact that I was already dressed in my blue tartan trousers, she held out a skirt and insisted that I put it on. As I argued against changing, she knelt down in front of me and held the waist of the skirt open for me to step into.

"We are going to visit a priest and you have to wear a skirt," she told me. "You have two choices, either you take off your trousers and put the skirt on or you wear the skirt over the trousers."

I was unhappy with both choices, but I was willful and didn't want to let Mum win, so I opted to wear the skirt over my trousers. I remember sitting in the car wondering what others might think about my strange dress choice.

It was the first time I'd heard Mum use the word "modesty," and I wondered what it meant. Since my brothers didn't have to put on a skirt, I deduced that this word only applied to girls, and I wondered why girls had to be modest. No matter how many times I turned it over in my young brain, I could not figure out what was wrong with girls wearing trousers. Mum never explained it to me, but from then on, I wasn't allowed to wear trousers, jeans, shorts, t-shirts or any short skirts, and to add insult to injury, I had to wear a scarf on my head in church, too.

In late 1975, shortly before my third brother, Richard, was born, my parents sold the Wendouree house and moved our family to a little house on a larger block of land in Gordon, a small country town outside of Ballarat. This was our first foray into self-sufficiency, my parents bought a goat who we named Sarah, and Dad quickly learnt that goats needed to be chained to a pole, preferably *away* from the clothes line or the cloth nappies would get eaten! My three younger siblings and I loved the new-found freedom we had to wander about the local countryside and explore.

Dad did shift work for McCain's Foods, so he was often home during the day and I have lovely memories of him helping around the house and making bread on the days he wasn't working. These were really happy times, our family felt somewhat "normal" and loving, apart from the extra praying and Dad was the happiest I ever remember. I attended school for the first time at the primary school just down the hill from our house. The school was so small that all the pupils were in one large room with only two teachers, one of whom was the principal. Having only been amongst family members until now, I felt very shy and socially awkward, and it didn't help that I dressed differently from other girls, and was always wearing dresses or skirts, no jeans, pants or shorts. My strongest memories of school are of being teased by other kids on the playground because the brown scapular that my mother insisted I wear, hung down below my dress. My schoolmates were curious and asked me what it was, but I didn't know how to explain what exactly the scapular was and why I had to wear it, so it made my school days and attempts at making friends awkward.

Just before Christmas, Mum gave birth to Richard and suffered a shingles attack afterwards and had to be quarantined in the hospital over the holiday season to recover. I remember my eyes being as huge as saucers when Dad took us in to see Mum on Christmas Day. The kitchen staff had put out a huge spread of every food imaginable, and it was more food than I'd seen in my life! During Mum's confinement, a couple that we knew through our Mass group came and helped out and then Matthew and I went to stay at their house for a little while, so that Dad was able to work. It wasn't long before Mum was home and life returned to normal. We only lived at Gordon for a short time because the house wasn't good for our health. It was very damp and moldy and because we were constantly sick, Dad and Mum began searching for another place to live.

Soon enough we moved to a little town called Waubra, which was in the opposite direction to where we had been living. This house was much better, had even bigger acreage, and my siblings and I loved this house even more! The house was an old white Federation style home with 25-foot ceilings, large bedrooms and a long hallway straight down the middle of the house. Every bedroom had a fireplace and, in one bedroom, there was an old-fashioned double bed that was so high I needed a stool just to get up on it! It was here that Dad honed his carpentry skills making pine beds and bunks, starting with his rapidly expanding family, and then making them to sell for extra money to supplement his wage. He stored the timber on either side of the six-foot-wide hallway, so everyone got used to walking around the piles of wood and with the comforting fragrance of freshly hewn pine that filled the house. Mum arranged for me for to attend the local primary school a few kilometres away, so I caught the bus there and back each day.

This school was a little bigger than Gordon, but I still didn't enjoy it much due to continued teasing. I still felt very much like a fish out of water and was impatient to get home so I could explore the property (and the surrounding paddocks), chase mice in the grain shed and play under the windmill with my siblings. It was a very happy, wild, carefree time.

During this time our family continued to keep strict prayer schedules and traveling two hours to Melbourne and back each

Sunday in order to attend Mass said in the Latin Rite. Dad hated the long-distance travel and the cost of it just to attend Mass, but Fr. Cummins had found a church in the Melbourne suburb of Armidale that better accommodated his growing following. I often overheard Dad arguing with Mum about it on the way home when we were supposed to be sleeping in the back of the car. Mum never seemed to have a practical answer for why we were making the trip and that made him mad. Dad felt that attending the local parish was just fine and with the expense of our ever-growing family, he keenly felt the financial strain.

It was at this church that we first met Brother Whittle, a religious brother who belonged to the order of Oblates of Mary Immaculate. Brother Whittle hadn't liked the post-Vatican II changes that his order had made either, so he still lived with his fellow Oblates and just attended Mass at Fr. Cummins church. He was a lovely gentleman who quickly became part of our family. He would visit at least once a week, bringing his elderly mother with him. We looked forward to his visits because he was interested in everything we did or had to say and always accompanied us on long exploratory walks, so we were able to venture further away from our house in the safe company of an adult.

In 1976, while we were attending Mass at Armidale, Mum decided it was time I made my first Holy Communion. Mum wanted to make sure I took the preparation of receiving Jesus for the first time very seriously, so she spent a great deal of time, many months in fact, teaching me the Primary Catechism. What it lacked in size was made up for by the volume of information that I had to memorise. All of the lessons pertained to the sacred truths of the Catholic Church, the Commandments and Sacraments. Once I'd finally worked my way through the book, Mum would often open it at random, ask me a question and wait for me to answer the question from memory. If I didn't, it was back to constant repetition until I could.

In preparation for my first Confession, learning all Ten Commandments and the sins against each one was equally as important as learning the catechism. There seemed to be a never-ending list of supposed sins that I committed on a daily basis and would have to confess to Fr. Cummins at my upcoming First Confession. Mum impressed upon me the importance of keeping my soul snowy white between my first Confession and first Holy Communion, so that Jesus would be happy to come into my pure soul.

My six-year-old innocence would be represented by the white dress and long veil I would wear, and whilst I was learning my catechism, Mum began making my communion dress. The morning she began sewing my dress, I watched as she carefully wiped the kitchen table, dried it, and then she gently lay out her white wedding dress and placed the pattern pieces over the top. As I watched her cut the fabric in long, confident strokes with the big sewing shears, I was still confused over the importance of "staying pure." I wasn't sure if it had something to do with keeping my dress clean or how it all connected to my soul, but it seemed to me that there was sin at every turn and women seemed to be at the centre of it.

Finally, Easter Sunday arrived. We rose early and Mum carefully hung my dress in the car for the long ride down to Melbourne. Once there, she and my Auntie Marie helped me change into my special dress, did my hair and pinned my veil on my head. They were both so excited to see me all dressed up, but I was more concerned with trying to remember all the instructions Mum had given me and absolutely certain that my dress stayed clean. Auntie Marie took photos of me, telling me to pose this way and that. I still have the photo where she told me to join my hands and look up into the sky pretending to see Jesus up there.

Mum had told me over and over that joy and peace would flood my soul once I received Jesus. I was confused when, after receiving Communion, I didn't feel any different at all. I'd been curious to taste the little white host and its bland and dry taste was a disappointment. When Mum asked how I felt, I dutifully kept my eyes lowered and told her I felt the happiness. Mum beamed brightly as she told me that now I was a Bride of Christ.

Shortly after my first Communion, Fr. Cummins moved his Mass community from the church in Armidale to an old building on

Hardware Street in the middle of Melbourne. I remember the street being quite narrow and the buildings very close together. I have no idea what this building had been used for, but it had at least three floors and a basement.

The numbers in the Tridentine group were growing quite rapidly and this was the most central place to have Mass so that the traveling time was equal for everyone. Auntie Marie lived here for a while, along with Fr. Cummins and Julie, (a woman who, Dad said, was as mad as a cut snake). I vividly remember Julie taking a group of children, my siblings and I included, down into the basement to kneel in front of a statue of Our Lady of Fatima that had been placed above some trickling water. I was too young to understand that this was actually a drain and not a spring containing sacred waters that could apparently heal. Amongst other stories she told us was that the statue of the baby Jesus was very special because it came alive at night and that she had seen it doing cartwheels down the chapel aisle.

Fr. Cummins traveled around a lot claiming he would go wherever he was needed, which meant that there was a rapidly growing number of Traditional Catholics dissatisfied with the changes in the church, and who were looking for meaning as they wished that life would revert back to "how it used to be." The congregation was made up of aging Baby Boomers who didn't understand modernisation and were afraid of technology, globalism and church advancements. As a result, they preferred to hold on to antiquated beliefs and the old ways of life because they were comfortable and familiar. For both my parents, and many others who were part of the Tridentine Mass group, it was much easier to revert back to "the old days" rather than push boundaries, explore new thought, learn, grow or be open to changes; both in the Church and the world, and as the world moved forward, the congregation stubbornly stayed stuck in its own little space.

It was around this time that Fr. Cummins had a unique statue of Our Lady of Fatima come into his possession. Our Lady of Fatima originated in 1917 when three Portuguese children claimed to have seen a vision of a woman dressed in white robes with gold trim who urged them to say the Rosary, pray for peace and then told them secrets that she warned them never to divulge. As word of the children's vision spread, the church investigated sightings of the mysterious lady, but it wouldn't be until 1930 that the Church would declare the visions "worthy of belief." Praying to Our Lady of Fatima involved saying prayers such as, "My God, I believe, I adore, I hope, and I love you. I ask pardon for those who do not believe, do not adore, do not hope and do not love you."

One of Fr. Cummins' requirements was that Our Lady of Fatima was to spend time at different houses, so he began a list of people who wanted the statue at their house. When it came our turn to host Our Lady there was much anticipation. Mum turned our little dining room into a mini-chapel, an altar Dad made stood along the wall with other large statues on pedestals. The one for Our Lady was dutifully dusted and ensconced with a pure linen starched doily and flowers. A child was posted as a lookout to let us know when Father was arriving, and the rest of us quietly followed Mum out, our scarves covering our heads, and began saying the rosary and singing Marian hymns to welcome the statue into our home. We were told that if Our Lady was happy with our behaviour and our prayers, then a beautiful fragrance would emit from the crown of roses on her head. We would carefully approach the statue several times a day to see if there was any fragrance that we could smell. I thought I caught a whiff of roses a couple of times, but looking back, I have no idea whether it was real or simply the power of suggestion. At the end of Our Lady's stay, each family who hosted the statue would dutifully report whether the fragrance was noticeable whilst the statue was in their home.

Fr. Cummins often stayed at least one night at our house during the week. He would arrive in the afternoon and say Mass early the next morning. Mum impressed upon us that this was a huge honour, and that our house and family would be especially blest because of it. Dad never placed much stock in this belief, he much preferred to have the house to ourselves but went along with it to keep Mum quiet. Dad didn't ascribe to the devoutness of Mum's religious practices, but despite the fact that he preferred to be out working rather than attending church, he followed along like the rest of us.

The night before Fr. Cummins arrived, Mum would carefully and devotedly dress the altar with all the obligatory linens that had been carefully washed and starched. In the morning, she would lay out the vestments in the precise order that she had been taught and my brothers would serve as altar boys for the mass. Other families who preferred the Tridentine Rite would come from round about to attend Mass at our house, and, afterwards, stay for a cuppa and breakfast. Dad was not only irritated with having extra people around, he was also irritated by Mum's insistence of kneeling in dead silence and ignoring all distractions for at least ten minutes after mass was finished in order to make her "thanksgiving" after receiving Communion.

According to Mum, it was disrespectful to eat so soon after mass, but Dad wasn't bothered by such things and so he would hurriedly gulp down his breakfast and then escape to work.

Fr. Cummins was happy to sit and talk, mostly about heavenly messages that had apparently come through the Virgin Mary from a seer in New York and foretold the End of the World. It was rather scary overhearing descriptions of chastisements that were predicted to punish us, but it was also reassuring to know that we Traditional Catholics were the "chosen ones" and if we were baptised and lived strictly according to the Ten Commandments, then we were almost guaranteed to be saved. These messages were supposed to be a comfort, in that we would be told what to do in order to survive the coming chastisements.

I remember a date being given for "The Warning," a dire punishment of a burning comet to hit earth, way back in the late 1970's. It was deemed "safe" for as many Tridentine Catholics to stay as close together as possible to support each other in saying prayers to stave off this dreadful punishment, so one night we slept over at the Hardware Street building in Melbourne. I remember getting up in the middle of the night to go to the bathroom and seeing all the adults keeping watch by the windows. Twenty years later, the memory of this potential disaster would haunt me.

Although Mum still won't admit it, this was the real reason she encouraged dad to buy the twenty acres away from town. She wanted to keep all of us away from the evil influences of the outside world, so she could home-school us and indoctrinate us in the Catholic religion in the hope that we'd learn to be self-sufficient, and while this was good in theory, the reality was very different. Keeping us safe from outside influences meant that we children formed no real normal friendships, and if we did, we faced the equivalent of the Spanish Inquisition regarding *everything* those friends said, did, read and watched so she could determine if they were suitable and our immortal souls were safe. Some of the kids we got to know from the church actually lived fairly normal lives. They attended local state schools, had friends in the outside world, played sports and watched television--all things we weren't allowed to do. Our lack of outside experience meant my siblings and I were quite socially naïve and frequently felt out of our depth when trying to communicate with other children.

In addition to talking about heavenly messages around the breakfast table, Fr. Cummins was often asked to bless special religious items. Father had a little black book that was full of blessings for every conceivable thing; tractors, cars, houses, renovations, farm buildings, crops, machinery, animals, to break drought, to ward off natural disasters and rid people of demons. When Father reached into his pocket and drew out his purple stole and holy water, we knew that we all had to be very quiet and reverent. At one point, Mum even had a serious conversation with Father about performing an exorcism on one of my brothers because she considered him extremely naughty. However, special permission needed to be granted from a bishop and since Father was a "rogue" priest, he was reluctant to push the boundaries in that regard. His reasoning was that if something went wrong, there could be all sorts of implications.

The End of the World prophecies permeated every aspect of our lives, even our exploratory walks round about the local countryside. Fr. Cummins had read in one of the heavenly messages that the only medicine that would prevent the chosen Catholics from contracting the plague, were the dried flowers and leaves from the Hawthorn bush. If you were unlucky enough to contract the plague, then the tea might save you if you had enough faith that you would be cured. So, every spring, Mum would send us out to bring back branches of flowering Hawthorn to hang up in the attic to dry. Later we would strip the dried leaves and flowers from the branches and store them in glass jars in the hope that their medicine and our faith would save us from the horrors of the plague.

I'm not sure how long we attended Mass at the Hardware Street venue before Fr. Cummins moved the Mass community to an unused motel in the affluent suburb of South Yarra. Although smaller, this building was much nicer than the city building, and it had room, for those who travelled a long way, to stay a night or two. Our family only stayed in the church/motel during Easter time when we had ceremonies for three days running. Dad never enjoyed these times, he wasn't comfortable in the city, much preferring to be at home on the land working.

Chapter 3 – Saturday

Over breakfast the next morning, while the kids and I talked about our plan of action, Tony remained silent. I'd told him that he had report to work on Monday at Goulburn and was relieved when he agreed to go.

I'd been married to him long enough to know what his tactics were, and I knew that, in his mind, he was thinking that if he just ignored the Sheriff's orders and prayed for a miracle, we wouldn't be moving. Whereas in the past, I would have felt sympathy for him and the fact that his life was about to drastically change, at this point I was past feeling anything for him. I was determined to get the kids and I out of this cult – no matter what. And I definitely wasn't going to allow him to hijack this opportunity for freedom.

Later that day, I left Tony and the kids at home and drove into

Nowra to fill the car with boxes before heading to the newsagent to buy a paper. The local paper was a few days old and I knew that the real estate agents closed at midday, but I thought at least I could have a look and see what kinds of houses were available.

When I arrived home, the house was a flurry of activity. The three older kids had swiftly and efficiently organized all of our possessions into three piles; a growing mound of rubbish matched in size by the charity shop pile followed by what we really wanted to keep. Aside from Tony, we all saw this move as the perfect opportunity for an overhaul of our lives and our possessions, and we were *not* going to be keeping any junk, and once Tony finally left for Goulburn, we had every intention of getting rid of even more stuff. It would be gone before he even realized it had been purged.

I did a quick read through the real estate section of the paper for rentals and realized that I had no idea what was a reasonable rental price nor did I know which area to look in. One thing I was adamant about though, we would move to a bigger house with two bathrooms. There wasn't going to be any more of this "living poor," if I could help it. I started by looking for properties in Cambewarra which was only a few minutes down the road. I felt comfortable in this area because I'd often visited the little shop and post office that Kamm owned.

Although I didn't want to have anything to do with him or the cult, it never occurred to me to completely break all connections and look further afield for a house. In fact, it made me feel a bit anxious just thinking about moving too far away.

Looking back on it now, I can see how, like a plant that is never repotted, I became conditioned to thinking and living small.

Chapter 4 – Falling Away

In late 1977, my parents bought a 20-acre property in Lal Lal (which means "falling waters" in an Indigenous language of Australia), which was 30 minutes outside of Ballarat. It had initially been part of a larger farm, but the owner, who was getting old, had decided to sell off the property in large parcels, and although it was only a couple of miles from the little town of Lal Lal, it was remote. We had no neighbors within sight and on one side of the house were paddocks of gum trees, leading down to the Bungal Dam, which provided Ballarat and Geelong with their water supply.

Dad liked the fall of the land and if he couldn't be an accountant, then it was his dream to have a small farm of his own and raise some pigs. Unfortunately, the local council denied dad's application to have pigs on this property because living near the Bungal Dam meant our land was too close to the town water supply. Our land had a small natural spring on it, which Dad got dug out to create a large dam for our own water supply, and he set up rainwater tanks for drinking as the dam water wasn't healthy for consumption.

Instead of building a new house, Dad and Mum bought a house in Melbourne and had it cut into three pieces, fit on three trucks and transported to Lal Lal. That year the ground was hard as a rock and the short yellow grass pricked our bare feet as we ran across it watching heat shimmering off the paddocks. Dad called it an "Indian Summer," and he spent hours out in the dry heat preparing the house site and digging all the stump holes by hand. He bought red gum stumps from Echuca and set them all out awaiting the arrival of the trucks carrying our house.

We were so excited when we finally saw the three trucks slowly making their way across the paddocks and we impatiently watched as the cranes, ever so slowly, lifted the pieces of our house onto the stumps. The first night we spent in the house was exciting, but when I woke in the middle of the night to go to the toilet, I panicked because I couldn't find my way out of the bedroom.

We lived in primitive conditions during those first weeks without toilets or running water. A couple of times a day, Mum would take us a mile down the road to the local park to go to the toilet. Meanwhile, my siblings and I had a ball helping Dad plaster, paint and add extra rooms onto the house to accommodate our growing family. Because the house was in constant need of renovations, we children became quite adept at building, plastering, cladding, painting, plumbing, concreting, tiling, roofing and (the dreaded) wallpapering.

In order to save on electricity, my parents decided to have a wood stove for heating hot water and cooking. A big stove was installed in the kitchen and was lit 24 hours a day, 365 days a year. This monster consumed an enormous amount of wood and as a result, it was unbearably hot in the house year- round, but summer was especially torturous. As each of my brothers grew older, they took turns ensuring that the wood box was filled twice a day, and Dad was always on the lookout for free wood to cut up and bring home to fill the woodshed. There were two hard fast rules about the stove. First, the flue had to be cleaned every couple of months. Second, and most imperative, was that only dry wood was burned since green wood would cause wet soot to cling to the flue which eventually dried out and caught fire. It shocked and scared us when this happened one day only a few months after moving in. We heard a noise like a jet taking off and when we rushed to the stove, the flames were roaring up the flue making the pipe glow red and exude enormous heat, and we were terrified that the whole roof would catch fire. After that we made sure only dry wood was burnt and that the flue was cleaned more regularly.

One day, whilst Dad was still in the middle of extending the house, we came back from getting the mail to see him in the back of the station wagon with his leg bandaged up. We rushed to ask him what was wrong. He told us that Mum needed to take him to hospital straight away. We were lucky that Auntie Marie was around to babysit us. In the short period of time that we were gone, Dad had cut his leg with the electric saw. He had reached up to cut a piece of framing and the guard had failed to close over the saw blade on the way down. When he looked down, the blade had cut horizontally across the top of his right leg almost to the bone, taking 100 stitches to close. Amazingly it barely bled as the blade had burnt the ends of the veins and blood vessels. I can't remember how long he was in hospital, but it wasn't long before he was back building again, albeit on crutches.

Besides extending the house Dad was kept on his toes building a cellar underneath the rumpus room, a large hay shed, milking shed, small pig pen, chicken shed and a small storage shed for feed. It wasn't long before Sarah, our pet goat who we'd gotten when we lived in Gordon, had more company with two cows, three pigs, a couple dozen chickens, a small number of sheep and four goats, who, over the years, gave birth to the most gorgeous little kids that made the best pets. It was such fun to have those little baby goats following us around! They were our favourite pets, and it was quite a sight to see them being bottle fed out near the back door, hungrily drinking as their little tails were going nineteen to the dozen! Having all these animals required a set of jobs that had to be done twice a day, so we were kept quite busy. During various times of the year we would be busier due to helping Dad cut, rake, bale and stack hay; drench, tail, crutch and shear sheep as well as helping out in the shearing shed down the road. There was always ongoing maintenance like putting up fences and gates, so those also became part of our skill set.

Only a few months after we moved house, my fourth brother, Clement, arrived in May 1978 increasing our family to six. Mum had decided to home school us, Dad didn't like this decision at all. Quite often over the years he would say, "Just send them down the road. It's only a couple miles away. There's nothing wrong with the little school down there." Mum resisted and said she was capable of educating her own children, but in reality our home-schooling education was *always* second on the agenda after Religious Education and this was first thing in the morning after breakfast for at least an hour. We had to sit on the floor whilst Mum preached passionately about the Commandments and the never-ending list of sins that could apparently be committed against each one of them. Before breakfast we had not only said prayers but had also learnt our section of the catechism off by heart before Mum tested us. We were forced to learn all the Catholic Catechisms by rote and not allowed to advance until that particular Catechism was memorised completely. Much like when I'd prepared for my First Communion,

Mum would open the book at random, ask a question and wait for one of us to answer it word for word. The older we got, the more we had to learn by heart, especially before a special event like First Communion, Confession or Confirmation. Mum impressed upon us the importance of always learning about our Faith. We needed to know it inside out and be able to answer any question that was put to us by an inquisitive outsider. It was vital if they were curious we be versed enough to convince them to become Catholic.

Our religious education also included learning to sing and chant Gregorian, the ancient Latin chant used for certain parts of the Mass and the office. From the time we were quite little, Mum would buy us a small missal so we could follow the Mass properly and as we learnt to read we were given a larger missal, Latin on the left, English on the right.

Our home-schooling curriculum was given the religious overhaul by Mum before we even started any school work because she was worried that outsiders would plant seeds of doubt that would lead to a breakdown of our faith and cause us to sin. Mum signed us up with a correspondence school operating out of Melbourne and we were sent each term's work about a month in advance. Although the envelopes were addressed to us, we weren't allowed to open them because Mum had to go through all the booklets first. She trawled through the book list that we were given for English and eliminated anything she deemed "modern." We were only permitted to read books that Mum was familiar with, which meant we were stuck with mainly old-fashioned authors like Enid Blyton, L.M. Montgomery, Mary Grant Bruce and a few other early twentieth century writers. Occasionally, if a new book was on the "must read" list, she would read it first to ensure there wasn't anything against the Catholic Church and, if it passed muster, she'd allow us to read it. Science was another subject that Mum carefully screened. She told us that dinosaurs were a figment of scientists' imagination and eliminated any hint of evolution or the Big Bang theory because this was definitely against the teachings of the church. "You have to be very careful of even the little ways that the Devil plants doubt," she warned us.

Despite Mum isolating us and herself, Dad involved himself in the local area right from the get go. He became a member of the Fire Brigade and the Community Hall, and got really involved raising funds, doing burn offs/back burns, upkeep of the trucks and equipment (in 2017, he received a medal for 50 years of service). He was on call whenever there were fires and since there are so many fires in Australia, he was always on call. One of my most vivid memories was when Dad fought fires on Ash Wednesday 1983, after a massive bushfire broke out down near Lorne, on the Victorian Coast, near the Twelve Apostles. It was so steep in places they couldn't get the trucks down, so the firefighters had to wait on the road for the flames to come up and fight it from there. Sometimes the flames or the fireball swept past them and went on up the hill. There was so much smoke the sun was orange in a smoke-filled sky.

Dad arrived home after three days of fighting fires without a break, and he smelt heavily of smoke. When he walked in the house, he told us that all he needed was to shower and sleep.

School day or not, come rain, hail or shine, our day began at 5:30am in order to milk the cows and goats, feed chickens and pigs, fill the wood box, separate milk, and possibly churn butter. Once those chores were done, we had to say at least half an hour of prayers before breakfast at 7.30am. Mum always made us say prayers before we ate because she said we would pay more attention to our prayers on an empty stomach. She also believed that fasting strengthened the spirit and quelled sinful desires. The latter was never clearly explained to us and we were even more confused when she told us about a biblical figure who rolled himself in nettles to kill "concupiscence of the flesh." Although Mum repeated the phrase on a regular basis, we never understood what it meant. Throughout my childhood, Mum used many phrases and words that we didn't understand, but she never explained them to us, so we were left on our own to figure them out.

Dad began his work day at 8am because, even though he worked for himself, he always liked beginning the work day early and having a routine, and he instilled this habit in my siblings and I, too. He wasn't formerly employed at this point, so he created his own income by making pine bunks and beds in the shed and sold red gum sleepers and posts for gardens that he delivered all around Ballarat and Geelong. Depending on the orders he received, we would take delivery of red gum slabs once or twice a month, and when we did a huge semi-trailer would make its way down the narrow road leading to our property and pull up on "the track," as our driveway was known. The huge stacks of red gum would be off-loaded all along the side of the driveway, and Dad would later deliver them to his clients. He would often take the younger boys, and they quite enjoyed the jaunts with Dad because he would treat them to ice cream before swearing them to secrecy. Almost every day we spent time helping Dad out in the garage making the various pieces of furniture, so we all became quite adept at using the drop saw, drills, electric screw drivers, hammers and levels (long before there were any safety guidelines introduced). Later on, Dad found employment with the West Moorabool Water Board and worked all around the Bungal Dam. It was at this time that Dad bought more sheep and these sheep provided us with meat and also some extra money from selling the wool.

To make sure we had a steady supply of meat, Dad found a mobile butcher who came out to our house once or twice a year to kill a few sheep and pigs. On the first day, the butcher would kill and hang the animals in big calico bags high up in the gum trees next to the house. I found the killing too gory to watch, but my brothers were right in there and delighted in telling us girls all the grim details at the dinner table. A few days later, the butcher would return to cut the meat the way Mum wanted it and we girls bagged it all up. One butcher's visit would fill our two large freezers down in the cellar with at least six months' worth of meat.

Another yearly part of our practical education was the bulk purchase of stone fruits from northern Victoria, usually collected on our way home from visiting Nanna, our paternal grandmother in Echuca. Once home we would spend the next week washing, sorting, cutting, stacking into jars and preserving all this fruit to eat over the next year. Any fruit that wasn't suitable for preserving was turned into jam, chutney or homemade tomato sauce. No food was ever wasted in our household because wasting food was considered a sin, so if we didn't eat our dinner we were served it for breakfast. If our morning porridge was uneaten, we ate it at lunch. That awful taste of thick, cold porridge drenched with honey and milk stuck with me, and it wasn't until many years after I left home that I could face a bowl of porridge again.

In our house, cooking was a daily task that was left to Mum. She had been baking bread for as long as we'd lived in Lal Lal and as soon as we were old enough, she began teaching my sisters and I how to manage this work. Since bread was a staple in our diet, we needed to bake at least three times a week. Every time I smell freshly baked bread my mind is cast back to those beautiful dark brown loaves that we would take out of the oven, allow to cool before cutting thick slices and topping them with homemade butter and delicious honey. You haven't lived till you've tasted that! There was no such thing as packet cakes in our house, so all our cakes, biscuits and slices we baked from scratch as well. Mum dutifully taught us girls to carefully read recipes, weigh all the ingredients and follow the instructions to produce delicious cakes and biscuits, which were enjoyed by everyone who visited our house. Mum took pride in her cooking, and she taught us that we were to aim for perfection in our baking and cooking because it meant we were thinking of God, but in reality our food was simple, plain, and boiled to death.

Feeding such a large family on a very small budget meant that Mum was always buying in bulk. Honey was one of our staples, so she found a local beekeeper who was quite happy to sell honey in 15-kilogram tins. Mum got it at a good price because it was unstrained, so we would often find bees legs and wings scattered through it, but it was too delicious for us to mind. A few years later when we were more settled at Lal Lal, Mum asked this beekeeper if he could teach my eldest brother some beekeeping skills. This gentleman was very happy to pass on his knowledge, so we ended up with a small beehive and fresh honey of our own.

Mum loved sewing and made many of our dresses over the years as well as her own. She was a very neat needlewoman and taught me to knit, sew and embroider. My younger sisters weren't as keen as myself, but I really enjoyed learning these skills. During my middle teenage years, I actually entered some of my needlework into the Ballarat Show and won prizes for my efforts. One project I was especially proud of was a replica of the Duchess of York's wedding dress that I made for a doll. The sequins took an age to sew on and I still have the dress to this day.

Despite the fact that we lived outside of town and didn't own a piano, Mum felt that she'd wasted her own opportunity to learn to play the piano, so it was her dream to have us all learn to play. When I was seven, Matthew and I began to take weekly lessons from an elderly lady in Ballarat. Learning the piano was fun at first, but as the years went by and the practicing became much harder and longer, we lost interest. No matter how much we complained, Mum didn't allow us to give up and, in fact, she actually bought a piano from Mr. Woods in Ballarat, so that we would could practice. At first, I resented the fact that I was forced to keep learning, but once I reached the higher grades and was able to play the more popular pieces, it was much more enjoyable. Little did I know then that all this musical knowledge would come in handy years later when I learnt to play the pipe organ.

I'm very thankful for all of the practical education I received because it held me in good stead all my life and when I had my own house, it not only allowed me to feed my family, but it also led to many a wonderful conversation over the kitchen bench as I kneaded bread, rolled out pastry, baked biscuits or made cakes. I've proudly passed these skills onto my children, too.

#

Looking back, I can see how my siblings were an essential part of the lessons I learned growing up. There were already five of us when we moved into Lal Lal, and in October 1979, on the day of my first piano exam, my youngest brother, Augustine, joined the family. He would be one of our greatest joys and also one of our greatest heartbreaks.

On the day he was born, Dad and Mum drove me into town for my piano exam. Unbeknownst to me, Mum was already having contractions quite close together. After my exam was finished, Dad dropped Mum off to the hospital, then drove me home. By the time he returned to the hospital, about an hour later, my little brother had arrived. When Mum rang up to announce the sex of the baby, I was devastated to learn that I had yet another brother. I felt we had quite enough boys in the house for my liking, and I'd had my heart set on a baby sister.

"I don't want him," I told Mum. "Give him back. Swap him for a girl."

"But he's really cute," my mother told me. "So much curly hair!"

"I don't care, give him back. I want a girl!" I insisted.

Mum got a bit upset, but she convinced me to wait till I saw him before I made my final judgement.

"Ok," I conceded, "but I want twin girls next time." I didn't have a clue how babies were made so it was a bit of a tall order, but baby Gus was definitely very cute, so I changed my mind rather quickly.

Nanna came down to look after us whilst mum was in hospital with Gus, as he affectionately became known. We all loved having Nanna in the house, she was our favourite grandmother. She was known to keep a lovely house and even though I was only nine, I was eager to learn! No day could begin till you had your "pinny" on, and as a result, she was never without her apron and a tea towel thrown over her shoulder. She showed me how to polish the copper hot water pipes till they glistened and explained how apples were waxed, so when you firmly rubbed them with a tea towel they shone in the fruit bowl. Next she taught me to rub furniture polish on the big wooden table Dad had made so it, too, reflected the sunlight. Even hanging out the washing was an art form for Nanna.

"You can tell how a woman keeps her house by how she pegs her clothes on the line," Nanna told me. Our house was spotless when mum came home and we'd all learnt new skills to keep it that way.

Each February we looked forward to our two-week holiday in Lorne along Victoria's Great Ocean Road. Dad didn't like the beach, so he would drop us all off and come back after a fortnight to pick us up. One of Mum's relatives, who we called Auntie Eileen, owned a house there and she used to let Mum have the bottom unit for free once the school holidays were over.

It was a lovely open two-story house with the ground level as a separate self-contained unit. The unit was *very* small, but somehow or other we all crowded in for meals and to sleep. We spent pretty much the whole day at the beach, just down the hill. We loved going to the beach, but there was no bikini wearing for us. Mum insisted on the full swimsuit complete with Madonna like cone inserts. Luckily the beach was almost empty because I felt so self-conscious in my beach wear. Once home we loved to sneak up the stairs to chat with Auntie Eileen, whose favourite pastime was to bake and tell stories. Her husband Jack, was a very grumpy old man who preferred to sit out on the verandah in his rocking chair and watch the world go by, so we tended to leave him alone.

One year our Lorne holiday almost changed our lives forever. I was happily playing in the waves when mum come to me with a very worried look on her face. "Where is Gus? Have you seen him?" she asked me. I felt my heart drop into my stomach. I hadn't seen him and quickly got out to start helping Mum find my beloved baby brother. No sign of him anywhere. I felt scared. My other siblings gathered in a subdued group on the sand. Mum began walking along the foreshore asking everyone she met if anyone had seen a little toddler. Someone found a small pair of togs, but thankfully they didn't belong to Gus.

Despite searching for what seemed like forever and not finding any sign of him, Mum decided to take us all home. We all trudged quietly up Bay Street, each busy with our own thoughts. We couldn't even imagine our family without baby Gus. How on earth would Mum tell Dad? What would be his reaction? We walked up the stairs to tell the bad news to Auntie Eileen. As soon as we entered the kitchen we saw our little brother sitting up at the bench, eating biscuits! That was the happiest sight ever! Since he was too little to tell us exactly what happened, we figured that he couldn't find us when he came out of the water, so he found his own way home. We were amazed that he hadn't gotten killed walking over the busy road.

At some point, Mum had decided that being surrounded by religious books and icons was not enough to keep us safe, so she made us wear religious items as well. At first it was just a brown scapular that supposedly had miraculous powers that would protect the wearer from committing a mortal sin thus eliminating the suffering in purgatory and assuring the wearer salvation. The brown scapular was considered special for our family after finding a story in one of the little books about an apparent "miracle" that had occurred the century before when John McAuliffe had thrown the brown scapular he was wearing, into a raging sea and immediately calming it. As Mum read more religious books and papers, she added extra religious items to our wardrobes, and in a few short years, there were so many medals and scapulars around our necks that Mum sewed us little pouches to hold them all, so we could wear them around our neck every day. Dad didn't like it at all, and he only wore the brown scapular under duress. Even then, he tied it to his clothing, never wearing it around his neck. He often told Mum that it was dangerous for us to have cords around our necks and that he feared us accidentally choking or being hung if the cord caught on something. As usual, Mum ignored his protests and went about doing her best to save our immortal souls.

Despite the constant focus on religion, there were times when Mum tried to involve us in what could only be considered "normal" activities. At one point, Mum thought it would be a good idea for my brother and I to learn to play tennis. Mum signed us up with a local club and, despite being complete novices, we were put straight onto a team. We hadn't a clue how to play nor did we understand any of the rules. This made it equally frustrating for the other team members because our side kept losing. I felt uncoordinated, and knew I looked ridiculous, but Mum wouldn't allow me to wear shorts, track suit pants or the usual tennis skirt. Instead, I was made to wear a collared, knee length skater style dress with sleeves to the elbow that Mum had sewn. I was so embarrassed that I didn't even want to show up on the court, but my sense of responsibility forced me to do so. Even though I didn't know how to play, I wasn't about to let the team down. One highly competitive girl left our team out of sheer frustration with our useless tennis skills. Needless to say, we only lasted one season and the whole experience ended up being humiliating and embarrassing

Mum often took us on trips to salvage things from convents or monasteries that were closing. I don't know how Mum got wind that they were closing down, but I do remember traveling out to Mt. Macedon with Mum and Auntie Marie pulling a small trailer. Since Vatican II had swept through the Catholic Church and updated teachings, the old books were deemed out of touch with the changing world and a group of religious brothers were cleaning out their library. Mum and Auntie Marie were horrified that these "treasures" were being binned, so all of us kids were coerced into helping fill the trailer with these books on Canon Law, Moral and Pastoral Theology, and religious retreat mediations. These books were for priests, not the uneducated faithful and as lay people, we had no use for them. Dad wasn't a reader in the best of times, so seeing bookshelves filled with even more books, let alone religious ones, didn't really go down well. Much to Mum's horror (and our amusement), he always threatened to pile them up in the back yard and burn them. Mum took the ¾ size religious statues and even found a life-size crucifix that, at one point, hung in our hallway. Mum said this would serve as a reminder of how much Jesus had suffered for us and how our sins hurt him. Each spring our job was to help Mum spring clean the house and Dad was required to carry all of the statues out onto the front veranda where we were then taught how to carefully scrub the them down with a soft brush and soapy water so that they would look shiny and new.

Sundays were the longest and most boring days. We rose at 5am in order for the boys to milk cows and feed animals whilst we girls organised breakfast and dressed the younger kids. Afterwards, come rain, hail or shine, we all piled into the car by 6am to set off for the two-hour trek to Mass. Mum would make us pray aloud whilst traveling, so the younger kids would often feign sleep in order to avoid having to pray. It fell to us older kids to keep up the responses in the back of the car. If we failed to answer, Mum would call back ordering us to "answer up." Closer to our destination Mum would begin our preparation for Confession.

We were considered a good Catholic family because we were the first to arrive at church each week and line up for Confession. The Act of Confession is supposed to be an admission of the sins you've committed and a way to make peace with God before you receive Holy Communion. Confession is supposed to be between the sinner and the priest, thereby leaving the choice of which sins to confess up to the one doing the confessing. However, in our family Mum would list all of our sins that we'd committed through the week and remind us of them on the trip down to Melbourne. Once there we'd dutifully line up under mum's watchful eye, go in to Confession and tell our sins to the priest, who would give some advice and a penance. This penance was a prayer, or a set of prayers given to us to say in order to make small reparation for our sins. My siblings and I liked to compare penances with each other to see whether the priest ever changed it. Mum thought it very disrespectful, so we did it secretly. Once Confession was over, we'd go off outside till the beginning of Mass. Mum got very irritated by our lack of desire to stay inside the church and pray (like she did) for hours on end. She kept telling us that we never "prepared ourselves enough for the great miracle of receiving Jesus in Holy Communion." Often, she would come out of the church to tell us to keep quiet and order us inside before it got too late because she liked us sitting up the front with her. Our plan was to sneak in just before Mass started so we could make a quick escape once Mass was done, and as we grew older this became easier to do. Invariably Mum would watch the Communion line for signs of us and afterwards tell us off for not being pious enough. We never seemed to escape her omniscient religious gaze.

Chapter 5 – Sunday

As things had grown more oppressive in the Order, I'd sought out a new parish where I could worship in peace and now I was eager to share the news of our eviction with the members of Berry parish. They understood what good news it was and were all so excited and supportive! My friend Cynthia, from the Kangaroo Valley parish, was particularly happy that, at last, we were going to move away from the cult.

She'd lived in the area for quite a few years and had many contacts, so she helped me by sharing the names of estate agents with me and even contacted people herself. She also suggested going to the housing commission and applying for money for the bond to ease the financial burden.

Buoyed by the parishioner's enthusiasm, my children and I set to more sorting and packing. As we went from room to room it became clear to us that, although we were ridding ourselves of a lot of junk, there was still so much more to sort through. On one of my trips to the kitchen I looked up to see Peter Jirgens, the owner of a local civil engineering business, outside talking to Tony. Tony had answered a newspaper ad that Peter had placed, and, over the past few years, had done work for him. Unbeknownst to me, Tony had mentioned the Sheriff's visit to Peter, so I was surprised to see the friendly, smiling face of Margie, Peter's wife, at our door. I'd never had the pleasure of meeting Margie, but I knew that her eldest daughter was in the same grade as Josh and that Margie was very involved in the school.

After introducing herself, Margie told me that Peter had relayed the news about us being evicted and that she'd come over with him, so she could offer her help. I couldn't believe it! I'd been surrounded by Catholics all my life who were supposed to be the epitome of all the Christian virtues, but in my experience I'd found them very judgmental and critical, and rarely willing to actually help. Yet here was a Christian from another denomination who was actually offering heartfelt assistance with no strings attached. This felt like another miracle.

Margie swooped in, took stock of the situation and told me that she'd cleared her diary, so she could come with me the next couple of days to look at houses. I felt a surge of relief. I had been worried about house hunting and felt a bit embarrassed by my lack of life experience, so I gratefully accepted her help.

That night I went to bed feeling more loved than I had in years.

Chapter 6 – Religious Education

A couple of years after Mum and Dad moved our family to Lal Lal, and not long after Augustine was born, Fr. Cummins found an unused Protestant church in the bayside suburb of Hampton, Victoria and moved the congregation out of the motel. The new church was turned into our central place for Mass (and is still being used for worship to this day) and was about 130 km away from our house. Fr. Cummins also rented the house across the road for himself and his religious partner, Brother Alban, who had joined the Tridentine movement a few years beforehand.

The church came with a large hall, which had a number of rooms in it. Almost before the lease was signed there were single people wanting to move in, so they could attend the One True Holy Mass every day. Amongst them, a few young men who were finishing up their studies before entering a seminary created by Archbishop Marcel Lefebvre (a conservative who had opposed the changes implemented by Vatican II) in Écône, Switzerland. The Catholic followers of Archbishop Lefebvre splintered from the church and declared themselves the Society of St. Pius X (SSPX), and Lefebvre spent most of the next two decades arguing against the modernisation of the Catholic church. In 1988, he willfully disobeyed an order from Pope John Paul II and consecrated four bishops. The following day, The Holy See excommunicated Lefebvre and the four bishops, and Lefebvre remained estranged from the Catholic Church until his death three years later.

Fr. Cummins, a devotee of Lefebvre, had contacted the Archbishop and been promised that as soon as the first Tridentine priests were ordained, one would be sent over to help with the workload.

Due to his interest in heavenly messages, Fr. Cummins also attracted supposed visionaries, who would come stay at the church from time to time. One such woman was an old Polish lady who spoke no English but collected myriad dolls from charity stores and lining the window sills with them. She appeared to appreciate visitors, so my siblings and I would go see her on Sundays. One Sunday we got the fright of our lives when she suddenly went from being all smiles to loudly wailing, flailing her arms about, and speaking rapidly in her native tongue. We couldn't understand a word she was saying nor any clue as to the sudden mood change, so we quickly disappeared.

There were quite a number of people who attended Mass, in and around the Ballarat area who found the travel to Hampton too far and too expensive. Despite the Catholic Church's strict teaching on Catholics attending Mass every Sunday under the pain of mortal sin, those in the Tridentine group were exempt. Fr. Cummins announced that because the Church had strayed from the original teaching that the Mass should *never* be changed, the Novus Ordo (the New Mass) wasn't valid. Therefore, it was actually better not to attend any Mass (unless it was the Tridentine Mass), so a good number of congregants around Ballarat were missing out.

Fr. Cummins asked my parents to organise somewhere suitable for him to say Mass once or twice a month and make it easier for them to attend the "true Mass." Dad found a local Scout hall in an outer suburb of Ballarat that could be rented cheaply, and Fr. Cummins began saying monthly mass there.

Mum didn't like going to mass here because it wasn't in a church and she much preferred the traditional church environment. Part of the problem with the new location was that it was quite laborious for our family because we had everything needed for the ceremony and had to arrive early in order to set up the portable altar (which Dad had made), set out vestments and sacred vessels, arrange chairs and kneelers for everyone, and then pack it all away afterwards.

It was one of these Sundays in November 1980 when my younger sister was born. We had prepared and packed up the car to take everything we needed for Mass. Dad drove us all to the hall first and Mum set up with some assistance from other ladies. Then Dad took her to the nearby hospital, where she gave birth to Annette later that morning. I was very excited to have another little sister at last! It was an extremely hot summer that year, so hot in fact that Mum had to borrow a portable air conditioner to put into the lounge-room to keep baby Annette cool. It was almost a full-time job to keep the ice up to it. Only a few months later Dad and Mum were able to go off for a couple of days well needed holiday. Mum arranged for another family that we knew from church to mind us, it was really only to have adults there because my siblings and I all knew how to run the farm on our own.

In mid-1981, Archbishop Lefebvre announced he was coming to Australia to visit later that year. Suddenly everything was turned up a notch because the Archbishop was going to perform the sacrament of Confirmation. The normal age for Confirmation was about twelve, when a child was beginning to mentally mature. The sacrament was to strengthen us spiritually against attacks from the devil but being so isolated we had no idea what devilish attacks to expect. However, we dutifully learnt the thick catechism along with all the other information under Mum's watchful eye. This would be the second time that I would be wearing a special dress, this time not for Jesus but rather for the Holy Ghost. Although Marisha was younger than the usual age for the sacrament, Fr. Cummins had pronounced that since we were living in extreme times younger children could be confirmed.

Over the next few months, the number of us scheduled to be confirmed grew exponentially until there seemed to be no age limit. Adults, who had already been confirmed by their local bishop five or ten years before, were now planning to be confirmed again. Because there had been so many new changes in the church since 1962, the Archbishop and Fr. Cummins engaged in a protracted debate over Canon Law as they tried to decide whether or not the bishops in the "Modern" Catholic church were able to confer valid orders and/or sacraments any more.

Before we knew it, Confirmation day was upon us. We arrived at the church early just so we could get a car park, there were people milling about all over the place, quite a few were strangers to us. I'd never seen a bishop before and the way people talked about him, I was in awe. Each person being confirmed needed to have a sponsor and this had posed more Canonical questions. We needed to be sure that our sponsor had been "properly" confirmed so Mum had chosen much older women to be our sponsors. There was no room in the church for anyone else besides the sponsors and their charges. We all filed into the church, filling it to capacity. The regular parishioners were forced to stand outside. Mum had instructed us on how the Rite of Confirmation was given, we had to respectfully kneel in front of the bishop and bow our heads whilst he invoked the Holy Ghost. Once that was done he lightly slapped you across the face to signify strength against temptation. I'd never been hit in the face for any reason so when the bishop slapped my left cheek, it shocked me, and I had to be reminded to get up and walk away. Mum had told us our minds would be flooded with the Gifts of the Holy Ghost but, aside from a stinging cheek, I didn't feel anything different.

After my Confirmation, the church continued to extend into our lives. Back at home Dad had built the little convent for Aunt Marie and then constructed a large shed that, on paper, was supposedly to be used for storage of tools and machinery.

Somewhere along the line it was suggested that part of this shed be used for a chapel where Fr. Cummins could say Mass, instead of using our dining room as we were getting more and more attendees. In addition, the Blessed Sacrament could be on display, enabling Aunt Marie to meditate for hours in front of the tabernacle just as she used to when she lived in the real convent.

We kids could see Dad wasn't keen about any of this at all, but he was forced to go along with it because Mum and Fr. Cummins pressured him until he gave in. In the end, three-quarters of the shed was laid out as a chapel and the rest of the space was used for storage of religious items (life size statues, altar wine and excess religious books). Fr. Cummins bought the altar wine in bulk and would then take a couple of bottles whenever he visited one of his many Mass centres. After the shed/chapel was completed, Fr. Cummins asked dad to find and fill two large fuel tanks that would be housed deep in the ground on our property. The purpose of these tanks was to store fuel for the End Days and ensure that Fr. Cummins could still travel to say Mass, since it was the celebration of the One True Mass that kept the world turning and staved off the chastisements.

We were surrounded by everything religious; religious education, life size statues in the house, Mass kits, altar linens, vestments, and a gazillion religious books. We even learnt to read Latin. Mum taught my brothers to be altar boys, instilling in them the serious nature of such a calling. Serving the Mass was considered the first step on the way to priesthood, and it was always Mum's desire that we at least "test our vocations" before considering marriage.

Saying the rosary was taken to a whole new level as well. My siblings and I were forced to kneel in a line in front of Mum who would be holding a wooden spoon. If any of us slouched or knelt on our haunches she would poke us, telling us to kneel up and meditate. It didn't matter that the floor was hard and cold, she said it was a small penance considering what Jesus suffered for us. I know it annoyed her that she couldn't control Dad's kneeling habits. He always leaned on a chair and put a cushion under his knees as he raced through the prayers as fast as possible. Mum wouldn't allow us to say the prayers in a hurry, though. In fact, she made us enunciate each and every syllable to show our respect for Mary and bow our heads whenever we said Jesus' name. After the rosary was finished, we would dutifully hang our rosaries on the hand of the Our Lady statue whilst Mum would praise the children she thought had said the rosary in a respectful manner.

In addition to all the praying we were required to do, another of Mum's obsessions that annoyed Dad to no end were the number of votive candles that she lit, and the fact that she often tried to keep them alight when we left the house. In Mum's mind, the burning candles showed our devotion to and faith in the heavenly deities, and she believed that when they saw how devoted we were, they would provide everything we needed and keep us safe. We got used to Dad questioning Mum before we left the house each time, asking whether she had extinguished all the candles or not. Mum never envisioned anything going wrong, so ever-practical Dad pointed out that if the house burned down, the insurance wouldn't cover rebuilding it.

Another of Mum's favourite practices was to keep an AU$5 note taped under a small Infant of Prague statue. Mum never tired of telling us that this act of faith would keep the wolves from the door, no matter how dire the situation might be.

We wouldn't run out of food, and there would always be enough money to pay the bills. Nevertheless, this practice didn't stop Dad from being stressed about money or Mum from constantly praying for more of it. Somehow there always seemed to be food on the table; however, aside from Mum, none of the rest of us attributed this to the Infant of Prague. We were able to hold our heads high since living right on the poverty line was considered honourable, and basically guaranteed us a higher place in heaven due to our sacrifices.

#

When I was thirteen, Mum decided it was a good idea for us four older children to learn ballroom dancing because that was good, innocent fun for teenagers. So, we began lessons once a week at a local studio. Although curious to see what dancing would be like, it was quite scary walking into the studio for the first time. Having been taught that outsiders needed good example from True Catholics and conversion to Catholicism, we were unsure what to expect, how to act and what to talk about. We felt very much like fish out of water and it took a few weeks of bumbling conversations before we began to know other kids.

Once that wore off a bit we relaxed and actually started to look forward to the weekly outing.

My sister and I really looked forward to Thursdays and dancing lessons, but it was imperative that we keep our excitement to ourselves, otherwise Mum would ask too many questions. We definitely didn't want her cancelling the dancing lessons because of the music. Sometimes Mum dropped us off early and we'd sneak down to the newsagent where we would read through the magazines trying to catch up on things we'd overheard the girls talking about. Other kids bought lollies to eat during their dancing lesson, but we never had any money for such frivolities.

Although we would chat with other kids there, it was quite awkward for us because we really had nothing in common and were still very backward on so many levels. The way we dressed didn't help matters any either. Whilst our peers were all keeping up with the '80's fashion, we were dressed in our modest neck to ankle hand me downs. However, the dancing classes exposed us to all the new '80's music and we absolutely loved it! It was definitely very different from all the classical numbers we'd been brought up on, and, as a result, we had to keep it a secret from Mum, since she frowned upon all this "new evil stuff." I well remember one Thursday afternoon when she arrived unexpectedly early to pick us up and Madonna's "Like A Virgin" was blaring. Our hearts sank when we saw her disapproving face as she walked in, we were actually beginning to thaw out and feared that Mum would stop us coming. She angrily demanded to know what it was and ordered us to turn it off, even though the studio didn't belong to us. We didn't dare tell her that Madonna's album was called "The Immaculate Collection," she would certainly call it sacrilegious.

On the drive home, she questioned us about the music that was played and wanted to know why the old familiar tunes she was used to weren't danced to any more. Dancing was a wonderful outlet, I thoroughly enjoyed it and became good enough to earn myself some private lessons and go for medals. My first crush, from afar, was a young lad who often helped out with the dancing lessons. I was only 14, and he was a year or two older. Due to accompanying his sisters to the studio regularly he was a much better dancer than I, and since I was so sheltered, I had no notion of how to behave around boys and didn't even know how to converse properly with them. He attended a local Catholic college and seemed all grown up and "cool," and next to him, I felt inept, awkward and tongue tied.

Around this time, Mum began mentioning to me that she was going to have a talk with me and despite me asking her what it was about, she was never forthcoming with details. Until one day when I announced that I was bleeding. Mum seemed to be caught completely off guard, hurriedly showed me how to use a sanitary pad and then organised for some private time for us to talk. I was still mystified as to the subject and why was it was so secretive.

I soon discovered why. Mum got out some medical books that she kept hidden in her bedroom and opened them to show me some diagrams of the woman's reproductive organs. I was completely taken aback by all this sudden information that I didn't understand and had absolutely no clue about. Talk of a holy act between two married people to bring babies into the world as God's gifts. It became obvious to mum as she continued her explanation that it was going completely over my head so she decided to make it crystal clear and that's when it got way worse. "Babies are made the same way that cows and bulls do it in the paddock." Now I was absolutely shocked and disgusted. Whatever this sacred sex thing was, I wanted no part in it whatsoever. Never. Ever. It was gross. Whenever dad had got the loan of a bull to service the cows, we were forbidden to look out the windows if they were doing "it." There were times when we were taken off guard and saw what was going on so when mum gave me this explanation of sex, you can only imagine my horror.

I would be almost 40-years-old before I was able to shake off this shame and disgust surrounding sex.

Chapter 7 – Monday

Three days after we were served the eviction notice, my three older teenagers assured me that they could safely miss a week of school, but I didn't want their absence from their studies to have an impact on them. So, I drove them to school that morning shoring myself up for a meeting with the principal after I'd decided to be completely honest with the school about what was going on.

I asked to see the Principal and, after a short wait, was led into his office. Gary and the entire teaching staff had known from the get go where we were living and I had made it extremely clear that I'd be moving as soon as the opportunity presented itself. Everyone had been wonderfully supportive in helping my children settle into their classes, and, for the first time, my children were actually enjoying school and, as a result, I was incredibly grateful for everything Nowra Christian had done. Gary greeted me in his usual friendly manner, and then I plunged into telling him my news. He listened until I was done, and then kindly asked if there was anything he, or any of the school members, could do. I told him that I was about to meet Margie to go look at houses, so there wasn't anything else that could be done right then.

"If there's nothing practical to be done," Gary asked. "Would it be alright if I prayed?"

"Of course!" I replied. I'd attended a few of the kids' assemblies, so I knew that the Christians just bowed their heads to pray instead of the whole kneeling down and blessing themselves the way Catholics did. So, when Gary closed his eyes and bowed his head, I followed suit. The words that came out of his mouth were so heartfelt and kind, I felt tears leaking from my eyes. I loved this easy way of just asking God for what you wanted and needed, it was much simpler than the Catholic way of doing things. I really felt like God was so much closer to me than when I kneeled in church and prayed to a bearded being in the sky.

After I finished at the school, I met Margie in town. She already had a list of possible houses that we could look at and we set off to look at one in Cambewarra. I felt a little down when I noticed that there were other people looking at it, as well, because I felt that I would more likely be the one that was rejected as I had more children than they did. Margie suggested applying for it anyway. I had prepared the paperwork and just handed it to the agent when I noticed that my application looked nothing like the others, and I felt embarrassed. I saw a strange look on the agent's face as she read over my application and I felt my face start to turn red. I wasn't sure of what I'd done wrong, but I knew I hadn't done it right.

Later I would learn that attaching a photocopy of my ATM card (thinking that was enough proof that I actually had a bank account) was one of my bigger mistakes, but at the time, there wasn't anything I could do about it, so I resolved to do a better job the next time.

Margie suggested that I widen my search to other areas of Nowra, but I felt uncomfortable in places I didn't know and, aside from taking the kids to school occasionally, I'd not even looked at that suburb. However, there was a new housing estate being built only a kilometer from the school and there were a couple of houses up for rent and since we needed a house within the next week, it would be ridiculous not to consider all areas.

So, off Margie and I went to look at houses!

Chapter 8 – The Memorable Years

In late 1983, we suspected that Mum was expecting another baby because she seemed to be getting fatter, but when we'd ask, she'd deny it. Soon enough though, her tummy took on that definite round shape and it became difficult to disguise! I was excited because I was desperately hoping for another little sister, and those last five months of waiting for my sister to arrive really seemed to drag. Mum had told us that the baby was due early May, so we eagerly got up every morning expecting to meet this new little person. When she didn't arrive on her due date we started to become impatient. Mum experienced some sciatica pain and hobbled around on crutches until our little sister Rosemary finally arrived on May 11. We all adored our new little pink bundle.

The next year, 1984, was memorable for many reasons. The first incident happened whilst my youngest sister, Rosemary, was still being breastfed. When Dad had renovated the house to enlarge it, he'd brought in an Oregon beam (a piece of wood eight feet by ten inches that was about three inches thick) and placed it across the top of two walls so he could extend the room and the roof line. We'd always been warned not to run in the house, especially down the two stairs from the upper kitchen to the lower kitchen and part of the reason was that the Oregon beam was fairly low.

One morning I came running through, thinking no one was around. Unfortunately for me, one of younger my brothers was hiding under the table and thought it would be fun to push a chair out in front of me. With cat-like reflexes, I jumped over it, hitting my forehead on the Oregon beam above. The result was whiplash and a two-inch cut across my forehead. I instantly ran into the lounge-room and slumped face down on the floor, almost giving my mother a heart attack due to the amount of blood flowing from my head. Mum quickly pulled Rosemary from her breast and called ahead to the doctors' surgery before we hurriedly set off for Ballarat. Thirty minutes later, I was lying on the table being stitched up by Dr. Murray who did such a fabulous job that when the wound healed I couldn't even see the scar!

The second thing that happened was that later that year I was "loaned out" to another Catholic family from church to help look after four children whilst the mother gave birth to her fifth. John and Betty lived down in Warragul, about four hours away from us. John had worked in computers in a city office before they'd moved to Warragul while Betty stayed at home with their children. We'd first met them when they lived in the Melbourne suburb of Brunswick. They had begun attending the Tridentine Mass in the days of Fr. Cummins and heavenly messages. John took these messages to heart and gave up his job because the messages had warned the True Believers that computers were the beginning of the dreaded 666 that would sweep the world. Reading this, John and Betty packed up to move into the country where "God would provide them with a house."

John's worry about computers and the dreaded 666 weren't completely unfamiliar to me. I remember when bar codes made their first appearance on products, Mum would definitely never buy products that had bar codes on them. The Virgin Mary had mentioned in her heavenly messages that the bar code was the precursor for the evil 666 that would eventually be forcibly tattooed on our foreheads in invisible ink. If we willingly accepted products with bar codes on them, then how much easier would it be for the Anti-Christ to announce himself to the world and mark us with our own special number? Mum was also very suspicious of ATM cards when they first made an appearance.

She felt that the government was closing in on us and keeping an eye on everything we did, and she felt that it was imperative that we stay under the radar as much as possible.

For John and Betty, God provided all right--a glorified hay shed on a remote farm outside of Warragul. John was not a practical person at all. In fact, he would spend many an hour just pacing up and down, lost in thought over anything from Beethoven's symphonies to his next move on the chess board that was constantly set up in the lounge room. He was always playing against himself, and everyone knew not to interrupt him or his game.

Although my own family was certainly not well off, I was quite taken aback at these living conditions. The building was open and roomy, but had only corrugated iron walls, which made it very cold in winter and extremely hot in summer. The family didn't own a refrigerator. Instead, John collected fresh milk from the dairy every couple of days and in between times the bucket sat out on the bench. Betty had carefully covered the holes in the wooden floor with corrugated iron before placing carpet strips over the top. Hot water for baths needed to be heated by lighting the burner outside. Being a very organised girl who was used to helping Mum manage a big family, I was up early to dress and feed the children, put the washing on and tidy the house. John was never a morning person, so everything was pretty much done by the time he got up. After my first few days, he decided that we should keep the work to a minimum by only doing one job a day; sweeping the floors one day and doing the washing the next.

Personally, I thought this was ridiculous. With so many people living together, the house needed to be cleaned daily. So, I just agreed with what he said and proceeded on with my own routine, having everything done before he got up. There was little he could say or do then!

I stayed with them for about three weeks and during that time I was with them I maintained the same religious practices that Mum had instilled but noticed that the McNamara's weren't nearly as strict about saying the Rosary and were quite a bit more relaxed about kneeling while saying prayers. Still, I was rather homesick and looked forward to Mass on Sundays when I'd get a chance to see my family.

#

I was going on fifteen when Mum went back to work as a nurse. Mum promised life would be much better as she would be earning good money, and this was very welcome as it seemed we couldn't afford a lot of things. She started working three evening shifts a fortnight, but all too soon Mum fell into the trap of working four nights a week. It would have been fine, except that me being the oldest, I was responsible for almost everything in Mum's absence.

Mum would leave at four in the afternoon and not arrive back home till almost midnight, so it was up to me to organise the afternoon jobs for the boys, cook dinner, bathe the younger ones and put them to bed, and then tidy the house. It was a lot of work for a teenager day in, day out. My younger siblings, who refused do as they were asked, made it even more difficult and Dad, who didn't have any input to the running of the house, didn't help lighten my load.

Around the time I was fourteen, Mum allowed a family friend stay with us on and off. Ken was a 27-year-old man who was quite lazy and had trouble holding down a job because he was unreliable and never on time for work. His bed was at the end of the rumpus room and one morning, when I went out to get a drink of water, he motioned me over. I had no inkling of what he wanted. He proceeded to passionately kiss me. I didn't know it was wrong, and what I remember was that while the kissing felt nice, I didn't have any other feelings for him - neither emotional or sexual.

I was completely unaware I was being preyed on. For the next few months he took every opportunity to kiss me and then one day mum caught him in the act. She was angry. At me. I felt scared because I didn't understand what I'd done wrong.

We'd been taught to respect and obey adults, it never occurred to me that an adult would do something to hurt me. She immediately took me aside and told me that girls don't do that. Nice girls don't go around kissing guys. Well I didn't know that. How could I know that? Mum spoke to him, but he didn't get sent away. Mum obviously told dad about the incident because that was when dad started to tell me that I was ugly, and no man would marry me. I didn't feel hurt hearing dad say that because it had never crossed my mind that I was pretty or beautiful anyway. Mum never complimented my sisters and I, otherwise we'd become prideful. And pride was one of the Seven Capital Sins, to be avoided at any cost (with the other six being: greed, lust, envy, gluttony, wrath and sloth).

Eventually, Ken moved on and settled in another town further away, and the only thing I remember about it was helping to make sure he took all of his things with him.

Despite the problems Ken stirred up, a few months later Mum invited another man in his mid-twenties to stay with us.

Tony was vaguely familiar because he was one of the young men who had lived and studied at Hampton in the early days before entering the seminary. Although brought up as a mainstream Catholic, he'd searched out Tridentine groups until he found SSPX and began attending Mass at our parish each week. Mum took a liking to him because he was quiet and prayerful, the added "bonus" was that he'd had some seminary training. During the months that he stayed with us, we learnt that he was the middle child of three boys from an Eastern European family and, that after leaving school at the age of fifteen and working for a while, he felt dissatisfied with his life and turned to the Bible. He was curious about ancient Christianity, which led to his desire to complete his high school certificate and learn Latin by correspondence. By the time his education was completed, he was old enough to be accepted into the

SSPX seminary in Switzerland, where he spent about two years. Not long after arriving he began to struggle with the strict regimen of study and prayer and, before long, he suffered a nervous breakdown. Despite various tests, no one could pin point the root cause of his ill health, and much like with Mum's psoriasis, when the Catholic Church couldn't find a clear reason for something happening with a novitiate, they solved the problem by deciding that Tony didn't have a vocation for the priesthood after all.

Despite the rejection, Tony was still convinced that he had a vocation of sorts, so he was sent across the border to France (where SSPX had a small monastery) and spent a few months there before being called home to Australia when his father unexpectedly passed away. After the funeral, Tony moved into the SSPX house in Sydney and spent several months as a religious brother, while his health became increasingly worse. Rather than treating the illness, the SSPX priests read it as the divine indicator and conclusive proof that Tony didn't have a vocation. After being rejected by the church and his community, Tony left religious life altogether, moved back home and took up waiting tables in a hotel in the city.

At the time Mum invited him to stay, Tony was looking for a change of scenery to move to the country and eagerly took up Mum's offer. This wasn't unusual for our family as we nearly always had someone staying at our house, we often had priests and congregation members at least visit. Mum was burning the candle at both ends, home schooling us by day and then heading to the hospital to work the night shift, so Tony seemed to be the perfect person to take over the job of home schooling and his seminary education made him even more attractive as a tutor.

Tony moved into the lounge room and the new routine began the next morning. Mum seemed to spend a lot of time talking to Tony because she had more in common with him than dad in the religious sense. It was strange to have someone other than Mum assisting me with my schoolwork, but over time we started to spend more time talking than doing my work. This was my first real interaction with an adult outside of my own family and Tony seemed to be genuinely interested in how I thought and what I said, and because I had no friends my own age to talk to or go out and do fun things with, Tony became my default friend.

During this time, Mum was busy with work and what had initially been four nights a fortnight turned into five nights a week. I was left to care for Dad and my siblings in Mum's absence and after all the work was done in the evening, I took to pretending to go to bed early, but instead of actually sleeping, I took the screen off the window and hopped out to go spend some time with Tony, who had since been moved to a small makeshift room at the end of the big shed not far from the house. The room had been a part of the chapel that Mum had had Dad build, but after the arrival of the SSPX priests (in 1982) who had refused permission for the Blessed

Sacrament to be kept on our property the chapel had been dismantled and was now used as guest's quarters.

As I entered my teenage years I'd not taken much interest in the outdoors because Mum had made it clear that things like climbing fences and getting dirty while out on walks wasn't considered ladylike. However, Tony liked to go bushwalking and he often asked me to join him when he was taking my siblings along. Away from Mum's constant criticism of my behavior, I found that I quite enjoyed the outdoors after all and was happy to go along. Spending time with Tony was all above board and innocent for me, I just wanted to talk with someone other than my family. However, my mother often pulled me aside after we came back and told me that she'd seen me hold hands with Tony because she had watched us through binoculars while we walked down the length of the property. I hated being spied on and couldn't understand why Mum kept telling me to stop holding hands with Tony and getting attached to him. I didn't understand the "getting attached" bit, since Mum had never explained love or the emotions it tended to generate.

For most teenagers, it would have been obvious that it was wrong for an older man to be interested in a teenage girl, but my mother's desire to isolate us from society had meant that she had also shielded us from important conversations. As a result, I longed to be normal but had no idea what that looked like. It's hard for people who are connected by technology and the Internet to understand just how isolated we were and how naive it made us all, but Mum wouldn't allow us to listen to the radio, read newspapers or use the telephone. She even threatened us with mortal sin if we ever read the writing on public toilet walls, on the rare occasion we used them. She tried to stop Dad from listening to the news on the radio, but he always liked to keep in touch with what was going on in the world. One day she wasn't quick enough to turn the radio off and we heard that a girl had been raped somewhere. I immediately went to mum and asked her what "rape" meant, as I'd only ever heard that term used as a crop name. She curtly replied that I didn't need to know so I went and asked Tony, but despite the fact that he was older and more experienced, even he skirted around the explanation, so I was still left wondering what was so bad about it.

Over the following months, I formed an attachment to Tony that, in my mind, signaled the beginnings of love. The problem was that without access to the world outside of my family, I had no way of determining what these feelings really were. I was 15-years-old when he started holding my hand on our walks and hand holding eventually led to him kissing me. I had absolutely no idea this was wrong because I was completely naïve about relationships between men and women. Although I'd been told about sex, actually having sex with a guy never crossed my mind, in fact, I didn't have any sexual feelings or attractions to Tony at all. When Mum discovered that I had formed an attachment to Tony she took me aside and told me that "girls don't do these things," but I honestly had no idea what she meant. It was also never explained to me that it was plain wrong for older guys to be interested in teenage girls, so all of Mum's warnings not only fell on deaf ears, they, quite honestly, failed to even make sense.

In my eyes, Tony was so grown up and more mature than my parents. He'd travelled a quite a lot, spent time overseas, worked at a number of jobs. The only other guy who I could compare Tony with was Ken, and when I compared the two Tony certainly seemed more stable. In my very limited capacity, I thought I'd be considered "mature" if I was with an older guy who had more knowledge of the world than myself. Never having had the opportunity to mix with other kids my age, I just took on a lot of Tony's thinking simply because I didn't know any better and he never encouraged me to be independent or to further my education. Being naturally shy and trained by my mother to be obedient, I thought the next best thing to do was to follow the course that seemed set out for me and marry Tony. He would look after me. We'd get married and life would be great. Or so I thought.

Tony stayed with our family on and off over a couple of years, the first time was when I was fifteen, the last time I was almost seventeen. During this time, he quite often adopted Mum's tendency of scolding me for not being ladylike enough. I laughed too loud, talked too much, crossed my legs, was too brash, too friendly (this could lead men into sin) and I danced too close to my male dancing teacher. Mum was often there when he said these things and she never stopped Tony from giving these "suggestions" because his priestly training meant that he knew what he was talking about. Even though she appeared to agree with Tony's way of dressing me down in order to inspire improvement on my part, she continued to order me to break off the attachment and yet never explained why or gave me a sense that I had other options. Tony told me he was in love with me, so I thought it was real.

As I neared seventeen, Tony began to feel awkward around the house and left to go live in Melbourne with his family again. We secretly planned to get married as soon as I turned eighteen, so he decided to go back to his original trade of boiler- making so he could make better money in order to provide for us. I missed him a lot, but that was largely because I'd become dependent on him and couldn't imagine what my life might look like without him in it. I equated life with Tony with being an adult, so, in my mind, life without him meant forever being a child in my parents' house.

Each week at Mass, Tony and I would find some time to sneak in a kiss and exchange love letters. I hid Tony's letters in my bra till I got home and could read them in peace, and I had to be really careful about hiding the letters as Mum periodically searched our drawers. This went on for about a year, and I had many letters from him that I would read over and over again. In my head this was true love because we were fighting against the odds and, according to the limited knowledge I had about relationships, true love conquered all. The reality was that a thirty-year-old man, who was already unhappy with his own life, was grooming an obedient and sheltered teenager to become his wife and was preparing to drag her into his well of unhappiness.

What's even worse was that, in an attempt to adhere to their religious beliefs, my parents allowed it.

Around this same time, Fr. William Welsh (from Houston, Texas) became our church priest. He endeared himself to most of the parish with his easy-going Southern drawl and friendly manner, but, from the start, I felt something was *really* off about this guy. It was the first time in my life I remember having such strong intuition. Whenever I was near him, I had this over-whelming feeling of suspicion and mistrust and I distinctly remember that it began on the first Sunday morning he heard Confessions. In the Confessional, I said my prayers, rattled off my list of sins, which included being "cheeky" (a sin Mum had always instructed us to confess because it translated to back answering authority and being disobedient) and waited for Fr. Welsh to assign me my penance. Instead, after hearing my confession, Fr. Welsh poked his head around the curtain, gave me a creepy smile and asked me what I meant by it. I was taken aback because no priest I'd known had ever been so informal in the confessional and it left me feeling extremely wary. Every other priest

I'd confessed my sins to had taken sin very seriously, and none of them had ever treated it as a laughing matter. I kept my eyes down and stammered as I explained, I couldn't express exactly what it was about him that made me wary, but from then on I avoided him whenever I could.

Mum opened up our home for the priests to visit anytime they wanted so it wasn't unusual to have them drop in sometimes. Usually it was planned though and they came for a meal. However, I vividly remember one day that both my parents were out and Fr. Welsh made a surprise visit to our house. He hadn't called beforehand like priests usually did and since I was home alone with my siblings, I did what Mum would do and offered him a cup of tea. He was overly friendly to the point of making me uncomfortable. I'm not sure who suggested going for a walk, but we all went out on a bush walk together. As we got further from the house he tried sending the younger kids on in front but wanted to keep my sister and I close by him. My sister quietly suggested to me that we run on ahead, just out of his reach, and keep our siblings in view behind us. We arrived home first and dashed to the safety of our bedroom, but just as we sat on our bed catching our breath, we heard footsteps in the hallway. Fr. Welsh had followed us up to our room! Our hearts were in our mouths as he opened the door. This had *never* happened with any priest and we were frightened, but before he could do anything, we jumped through our first-floor bedroom window and escaped. It was obvious that he was annoyed that we'd thwarted his efforts, but we were relieved that we were safely away from him, and, from then on, we kept a safe distance from him.

About a year after this episode, Fr. Walsh was notified by his superiors that he was being posted to India. He was openly unhappy about the decision and expressed this unhappiness every chance he got. One of the last Sundays that he was in Melbourne, he caught me walking past one of the bedrooms in the hall next to the church. Since many of the parishioners travelled from long distances away, they would gather after Mass for a cuppa and chat at our house, so, this time, there were plenty of people around. Fr. Welsh told me that he wanted to see me for something, but I could *not* think why on earth he'd want to speak with me, so, figuring that there would be strength in numbers, I insisted that he see my sister and me together, but he wouldn't hear of it. After arguing with him for a few minutes, my teachings about obedience to authority overrode my resistance, and I reluctantly went into the bedroom alone. I was very afraid because I had no idea what he wanted, and when he told me to sit on one of the two beds everything felt frighteningly close. So close, in fact, that when he sat down on the other bed, our knees were almost touching and I moved away. He gave me a creepy look and proceeded to tell me how sad he was about the decision to be moved to India and that he had wanted to stay in Australia. He said that since I was very special to him, he would miss me most of all. He'd not shown me any special consideration before now and I couldn't imagine why the sudden display of emotion, but he continued by assuring me that he would write me on a regular basis and ask his superiors to send him back. I felt sick to my stomach. I couldn't understand why I'd be special to him since not only did I dislike him, but also, I didn't trust him. As soon as I left the room I forgot all about it, and, thankfully, it was the last time I ever saw him. Years later I was horrified to discover that he had sexually abused quite a few teenage girls in the parish.

Not long after Tony went back to live in Melbourne, we had another male visitor in the form of Jeff Peek. I had last seen him almost ten years previously when he had visited from New Zealand with his cousin Diane and stayed at the Hardware Street building. His older brother, Frank, was one of the first young men from the Pacific to be trained and ordained by SSPX and then sent back to Australia. Jeff was looking for a good Catholic girl to marry and have a big family with and since I was the daughter of one of the founding families of the Tridentine movement in Australia, I was a prime candidate. Jeff played the guitar and was excited to know that I played the piano so that was something we had in common. He also joined my siblings and I on bush walks around our property. On one of these walks he tried getting a little cosy with me and since I felt nothing for him, I didn't understand why and I gave him the cold shoulder in order to keep my distance. Luckily, he only stayed a few days so there weren't any more awkward moments. A few weeks later, after I'd completely forgotten about him and his visit, a letter arrived from New Zealand and I was shocked to read that Jeff actually had planned to marry me. I'd already set my heart on marrying Tony, so the idea that another man would want to marry me never entered my mind. Even though Tony had not yet formally asked me to marry him, I saw myself as already promised to him and couldn't imagine looking at another man.

Mum was at work when this letter arrived and never saw it, which was a minor miracle since she examined and read every single piece of mail that came to the house whether it was addressed to her or not. Instead, I showed it to my younger sister and together we answered it, telling Jeff that I'd said yes to Tony already. I thought that would be the end of the incident, but when I answered the phone one afternoon a few weeks later (whilst Mum was at work) and heard Jeff on the other end calling from New Zealand, I was shocked. He asked to speak to Mum and when I asked why, he replied that he wasn't happy with my response to his proposal. When I repeated that I was marrying Tony, he seemed happy with that and hung up. Unbeknownst to me I'd not heard the end of it. He called again, this time when Mum was home, and they spoke in hushed tones for a couple of hours. When the phone call ended, Mum was not happy, and she berated me for turning down his offer of marriage because she felt he was a better catch than Tony, since he was "only" eight years my senior. I protested, saying that not only did I not like him, but I didn't want to go live in New Zealand, where I knew no one. Mum shrugged off my protests saying she couldn't see why I wouldn't take up such an offer. I believe she was so eager to break up Tony and me that she considered this her only option.

When I look back at this period in my life, I can see the way in which a lack of education and exposure and the teachings of the church combined to create an obedient young woman who had to rely on her instincts to figure out who was safe and who was not. Without someone to talk to about healthy emotional, social and sexual relationships between men and women, I was left to my own devices to try and figure out how it all worked, and, unfortunately, my system was not infallible.

Chapter 9 – Tuesday

After getting the kids off to school I met Margie again to inspect a few more houses. We looked at a couple in the Worrigee area, and I particularly liked one house. It was a two- story brick on a rise that had been a display home when the estate was first being built. It overlooked the town, and I could see hills in the distance. It was so new, so bright and airy with two bathrooms, three toilets and a dishwasher.

I was stunned by how perfect it would be for us, but I didn't allow myself to get my hopes up too high. I had no idea if I'd be able to swing the rent and I still wasn't sure about the area, it just seemed so far away from where I'd spent the past decade.

Despite the fact that I'd been desperately unhappy in the house

Kamm owned and the community, it was still scary to think about leaving everything familiar behind and uprooting my kids when I knew very little about the outside world and how to navigate it.

However, the house wasn't far from the school, which, for me, was a big plus.

That same day, I went into the Housing Commission and explained my circumstances. There was so much paperwork to fill out, and I needed help answering some of the questions. Applying for rentals was hard work and required a steep learning curve, but I was determined to do whatever it took so we could move. After all the paperwork was completed and the Housing Commission representative had had a chance to evaluate it, they told me that I was eligible for support and that all I needed to do was let them know when my application had been accepted and they would transfer the bond over to the agent.

I left the office feeling more hopeful than I had in ages, and relieved to know that we had the support we needed to find a place to live. Now I just had to secure the new place and make arrangements for the actual move.

We had exactly eight days before we had to be out of the house.

Chapter 10 – Growing Up and Getting Out

Life at home was a very isolating and our lives followed the same boring routine over the years because, aside from church and the arrival of new siblings, there was never anything exciting to break it up. The year round needs of our milking cows and other animals combined with our large family and a lack of extra cash for vacations, meant our school holidays followed the same routine as every other day of the year. It was only occasionally that we would be allowed to have friends stay with us and as we grew older, even less. With Mum working
full-time again, running the house was left up to me, and it ran well

because I was organised and responsible. So much so, that I was able to assist my younger siblings with their schooling as well as doing my own.

When I turned sixteen, it was time to do my work experience. In Australia, students in grades 9 and 10 are required to complete short-term work experiences in order to be prepared for the workplace and to explore possible career options, and kids who were homeschooled were no exception to the rule. From the time I was little, all I talked about was being a nurse, so I decided to do my work experience in the Queen Elizabeth Geriatric Home where Mum worked. I'd read every nurse book that I had been allowed to get my hands on and was really looking forward to work experience. One of the clear-cut rules of work experience was that students were there to observe and watch other people work, they were not to be doing work they had not been trained to do. I don't remember hearing this, though, I just wanted to help people get better, so it came as a very rude shock when, on day one, I was placed in the dementia ward and then locked in with patients who were intellectually disabled.

I had never come in contact with anyone who was intellectually disabled and, without any training, I was way out of my depth. My sheltered upbringing, which had constantly emphasized propriety and modesty made me feel very nervous and uncomfortable when I was asked to assist with showering the patients. Overhearing the nurses talk so openly about everything I had been taught was "rude" caused me to blush bright red. After a week of work experience, I was very confused about my life direction. I'd set my heart on being a nurse and the past week had completely shattered my dreams. This wasn't how I'd envisioned nursing at all, and I didn't know what to do or who to turn to for help. Mum was too busy to take me aside to chat about it and there was no one else to guide or advise me about what to do after my work experience. Mum disapproved of me attending University because she feared I'd "lose my Faith" because there was too much exploratory and expansive thinking happening on Uni campuses. She also objected because nurses were being asked to assist with abortions and, as a True Catholic, I couldn't be a party to that. I returned to my home-schooling feeling quite directionless, which only served to push me emotionally closer to Tony.

In 1987, after all the dancing lessons, I was scheduled to make my dancing debut in the very first Ballarat Begonia Festival Debutante Ball and I was very proud to be a part of it. Being homeschooled posed a small problem because I didn't have a partner and Tony wasn't in town at the time (not that it would have been appropriate or acceptable to allow him to escort me anyway), so Mum asked Damien, the same-age son of family friends, to be my partner. He agreed, and we took ballroom dancing lessons together for about six weeks with a dress rehearsal a couple of nights before my big debut. Finding a dress for the debut had been a challenge, not because I wanted a certain style, but because our restrictive Catholic upbringing prevented me from wearing anything that didn't literally cover everything but my head, hands and feet.

Finally, we found a dress that fit all the requirements and my excitement grew as I looked forward to the event. Mum did my makeup that night because she was so paranoid about me looking too "dolled up," and the result was that I looked like I wasn't wearing any makeup at all. My debut was yet another example of how I constantly walked the line between past and present, child and grown-up, and as a result, I didn't allow myself to fully enjoy the night because I felt guilty about not having Tony as my partner, which was totally unfair to Damien.

After my dancing debut, I continued on with my piano lessons and ballroom dancing in addition to my home-schooling, but it all felt pointless when I had no idea what to do next, so I decided to finish at Year 11, and then leave home and go live in Melbourne. I didn't have a clue what I would do there, I just wanted to be closer to Tony. I also strongly felt that if I didn't take the chance to leave home at this point, I would be stuck there forever. So, I began looking in the country paper for ads placed by people looking for a nanny and applied. By February 1988, I'd successfully landed a job as a nanny for a Jewish family in Caulfield, Melbourne. Mum wasn't happy that I was leaving home to take a nannying job, but since she hadn't offered any other suggestions I was determined to leave. She took me to the uniform shop to buy uniforms to nanny in and I went along with it, not knowing any better.

This nanny job was my first foray into the world outside of my family and Church community and I found it difficult in many ways. I'd not been exposed to any different cultures and knew very little about the world. A few days into my first job, my employer mentioned that it was fine to dress in jeans and a t-shirt, but I was still staunchly Catholic in my thinking that jeans were immodest, so I continued wearing my uniforms. In Melbourne, I stuck out like a sore thumb everywhere I went whilst looking after my charges. When the American wife openly expressed how much she missed her homeland, I couldn't and didn't understand. She was a very unhappy woman and spent most of her days outside the house while I looked after the two young boys. Upon her mentioning that she might kill herself one morning, I still didn't comprehend someone actually doing that. Mum had taught us that it was a mortal sin to commit suicide and those people didn't go to Heaven because it was a choice they made. I had no understanding of the mental torment that some people endure, and when I think back to that time with the knowledge I have now, I cringe at my naivety and the pain my employer must have been feeling.

After six weeks of low pay and very long hours, I left the nannying job and went on to work for a sock company on the production line. I didn't enjoy this factory job at all, since it involved sitting at the machine and sewing the toes of hundreds of socks. I tried to go as fast as could but never seemed to reach the quota. Once again, I felt very out of my depth because all the girls knew each other and I was, again, the outsider. The factory was in a low socio-economic neighborhood and attracted women who were rough, foul-mouthed, smokers who lived in poverty.

The cliques in the factory served to reinforce the sense that these women knew they'd never get out of the grinding poverty, and it was my first experience in such an environment. When I mentioned that I was engaged to be married, I foolishly thought that they would consider me grownup and include me, but that didn't seem to make any difference.

I was an outsider in too many ways.

Chapter 11 – Wednesday

I woke up and realized we only had a week left!

The days were flying by. On the one hand I felt excitement and, on the other, anxiety. I kept hoping that all the work I was putting into searching for houses would pay off and we'd have an answer by the end of the week. It made me anxious not to know what was going to happen, but with so much to do to get us ready to move out, I had to put the worry aside and get packing.

This was the first time in my life that I was actually in charge--of everyone and everything. Taking charge was a bit scary at first because Tony had always told me that I was useless at making decisions. This meant I kept second guessing myself while looking at houses and considering different areas.

However, with him away in Goulburn, I had a bit of peace, both mentally and physically, and, for that, I was thankful.

In the morning, I would get the kids fed and off to school before starting to pack and clean. Each afternoon, the kids rushed into the house eagerly questioning me about my day and whether I had been successful in getting a house yet. Even though I felt anxious inside, I kept my answers positive and happy because I believed that what you put out into the world, you got back.

Somehow, somewhere a house *would* become available for us, we just had to have faith.

And since we had to be out of the house no matter what happened, the only thing to do was continue packing and preparing.

Chapter 12 – Thursday

With six days to go, burning the candle at both ends was tiring and I was exhausted from packing and preparing a house move while continuing to look for a house for all of us. A bit unsettling really but I was very thankful to have this chance of freedom, believe me.

For quite some time I'd felt the inner stirrings of change. Now, my marriage was over in all but name, and I'd been ostracized by the cult members. Being ostracized didn't bother me in the slightest, in fact, I found it quite amusing to call out a cheery hello and see the shocked confusion on their faces!

Having spent the past decade of my life inside the community, I knew the thoughts that were running through their minds, "Should I return the greeting? Or not? We've been told she's a Devil Woman!"

It never failed to make me chuckle.

I'd tried sharing my thoughts and findings with others, but they were too deeply entrenched in Kamm's teachings and felt threatened by what I had to say and the fact that it might contradict the teachings they clung to. I knew that there wasn't anyone that I would keep contact with once I moved, and shedding the need to keep in contact with anyone from the cult gave me an added sense of freedom.

Despite the fact that we were facing eviction and had not found a house to move to yet, I felt a certain relief that my time in this cult was over. Each night I slept better, and every morning I looked forward to what the new day would bring.

I had no idea what it would really be like living in the suburbs, but I knew without a doubt that it *had* to be better than here. For me moving forward was imperative, if I made a less than perfect decision, then I'd just reverse it or take another direction.

Chapter 13 – Moving Away from Home and Toward Marriage

After leaving my nanny job I needed a place to stay.
Tony found a family through work and asked them to put me up, but they had six kids and I felt very awkward and out of place, so I tried to avoid spending time at the house. It wasn't long before I moved again to share space with an older single mother who had a couple of kids. I found it difficult to get on with her as she was a lot older and we were worlds apart in life experience. This venture also didn't last long before Tony suggested to his mother that I live there with her, Tony and John, Tony's younger brother.
I was glad to be under the same roof as Tony because it meant that I

didn't have to rely on him to pick me up or take me places all the time. He had suggested I not buy a car of my own because with a wedding to save for it seemed like a waste of money, but without a car, I was, again, isolated and felt like everywhere I went to live I was out of place and didn't belong. At my future mother-in-law's house, there was no spare room, so I shared the double bed with her and John didn't make me feel welcome with his abrupt, dismissive, off-hand comments, so I felt like I wasn't wanted anywhere. I certainly understand now how weird the situation was for them, but no one talked about it or offered to help me find a direction to follow. Tony and John didn't get on either, which didn't help matters, and John often told Tony off for the stupid things he did and ridiculous decisions he'd made in the past. They even had an argument just before the wedding where Tony told John to forget about being his best man. It made me feel even more uncomfortable and anxious, I urged Tony to sort it out otherwise there'd be a big family rift.

In order to earn money for the wedding, I'd gotten myself a job as a checkout chick at a supermarket across the road, which allowed me to walk the short distance to work and back. I enjoyed this job much more as I was involved with the public and I worked with many more young people. However, I still felt out of my element because the other girls were all very confident and up-to-date on fashion, movies, music and how to be teenagers. The young girls working there were amazed that I was engaged to be married at such a young age to a guy so much older than I was and, again, in my naivety, I still didn't understand that anything was wrong or strange.

After working at the supermarket for a while, I decided I wanted to be more independent, so I asked Tony to teach me to drive. He began instructing me in his work utility vehicle. After a few lessons, I was quite proud of myself and my confidence inched up a little bit. However, one day as I turned left onto a busy street, I didn't turn the steering wheel quick enough. The tire caught on the curb and the car hit a pole, denting it along one side. I was scared stiff and shaking as I sat there in the driver's seat; however, Tony was extremely angry. Without inquiring about my physical or mental state, he ordered me out of the car so he could drive home. I cowered on the passenger's side, my heart going at a rate of knots and apologising profusely the whole journey home, but he refused to look at me and completely ignored my apologies. When we arrived home, he marched on ahead and proceeded to freeze me out for the next 24 hours. Every year for the next several years, he signed for and pocketed my tax return as payment for the damage I caused, despite the fact that he sold the car shortly afterwards.

Although we'd talked about marriage, Tony had never actually proposed, so I brought the subject up one night. As I wasn't yet eighteen, he thought it'd be better to wait until my birthday, in April, to announce our marriage, but that wouldn't stop us getting engaged beforehand. I still insisted he ask me, so he offered a mumbled question right then and there. Even though I was hoping for a really romantic proposal, deep inside I knew he wasn't going to do any better. I accepted his proposal and we travelled into the city to look for a ring.

Tony had openly said that he didn't see a need for an engagement ring. His view was that it was an unnecessary cost and an overly modern idea, adding that he liked to be old- fashioned. I expressed real disappointment about not having a ring, so he reluctantly agreed to at least look for something small and cheap. I remember feeling empty inside whilst looking through the jeweler's window and checking the prices before looking at the ring. I finally found a small gold ring with a tiny diamond that he agreed to buy and when I put the ring on my finger, I felt so grown up. When we got home, Tony didn't say anything to his family, but his mother noticed the ring on my finger and asked him about it. He didn't act excited. Instead, he just shrugged his shoulders and told her we were getting married. She was excited because she had thought that Tony would never marry and had lost hope of him ever amounting to anything after failing to become a priest and then drifting from job to job. Now it seemed he had a purpose.

Tony told me that he wouldn't ask my parents for my hand in marriage because he was sure they would say no, so the first they knew of it was the Sunday after my birthday. We arrived at church and I announced my engagement to my siblings who had come running to the car when we pulled up. They in turn took off to tell my parents. Dad took the news in stride and was still friendly as usual, but Mum was very cold. The rest of the parishioners that I'd known for years were all very happy, so I didn't let mum's cold attitude dampen my excitement.

During the months before the wedding, Tony and I "courted." Having not been exposed to any form of normal living, I didn't know what to expect when you dated a guy, but even before we were married I felt that my relationship with Tony was somehow lacking. I'd read about and heard from other girls, the romantic dates they went on and wanted to experience that for myself. Tony never seemed to be excited about going out with me, unless it was to the movies where he could sit in the darkness and not talk. I longed for us to plan our wedding together because I'd read that other couples had done that, but he took minimal interest in the wedding plans because, for him, it was just about getting married as cheaply as possible. His only interest was in ensuring the church side of things were done properly. According to those who adhere to strict Catholic beliefs, as long as you have a lovely religious ceremony, then your marriage will be richly blessed and successful. You must also pray to accept "all the children God sends" because even though it might be a struggle, you will be highly rewarded in heaven. So, while I did the work of planning all the things that would make the ceremony nice,

Tony ignored me and arranged the service.

I hadn't gone back home for a visit since I'd left in January, so a few months after our engagement Tony suggested we visit my parents in an effort to smooth things over. Dad and my siblings were fine, talking away like normal while Mum quietly ignored us. It had always been hard to know what her moods were about because she always seemed to be stewing over something and when I was growing up there had been points when she hadn't talked to anyone for days. I approached her while she was at the stove to chat and managed to get some conversation going. She suddenly burst out with "Marriage isn't all happy you know. Before long you'll be bringing Tony his pipe and slippers whilst you look after the kids." In my youthful naivety I didn't believe her, I thought I could change Tony if there was ever a need to. She never once explained to me the host of things we had working against us, not the least of which was the fact that a thirty-year-old was an inappropriate match for an eighteen-year-old teenager.

A few months before the wedding, I began to feel really anxious about going through with the marriage. From the time I turned sixteen, marrying Tony was all I had thought about and now, suddenly, I had all these doubts. I chalked it up to nerves and uncertainty. I'd never heard about anyone ever calling off a wedding. Was it even a thing? I had no best friend or anyone who I could talk with and figure out my thoughts and feelings, so I did what I'd always done, and I kept them to myself. My biggest concern should have been myself, but instead all I thought about was Tony and how he would feel if I broke things off. How would his life be without me in it? I couldn't embarrass him and ruin his life like that.

I'd listened to my intuition when Fr. Welsh was being weird but I didn't connect the dots when it came to this major life decision. It never occurred to me that I actually *had* a choice, so I brushed off the questioning thoughts and ill feelings. From a very young age I'd been taught to sacrifice myself for others; that sacrifice was the highest form of love. As I thought about the wedding, I was only thinking about Tony's happiness, never of my own. I also the lacked self-confidence and self-esteem to venture out on my own because I had absolutely no idea what I wanted to do or even where I wanted to live. I was afraid to try life on my own and naively thought that everything would change after the marriage when we finally lived on our own.

#

Three weeks before our wedding, the wedding banns were duly read from the pulpit before the sermon. During those three weeks, we attended the obligatory pre-marriage information sessions given by, you guessed it, a priest. Although I recall very little from these sessions, there is one thing I could never forget. Fr. Hogan made it very clear that a woman must never refuse her husband the "marriage act", no matter how she felt or how many children she may or may not have had. And a man's seed must never be spilled because it was a potential child, a soul for Heaven. He did mention that a man must warm a woman up a bit, to which Tony nodded his head. I, however, was totally oblivious to what it meant.

The wedding day was a bit of a blur really. I was so eager to be seen and treated like an adult that I just wanted it over as quickly as possible. I spent the night before the wedding at my sister-in-law's and I dressed there with half of my wedding party whilst the rest, my younger sisters, prepared at home with my mother. Tony's uncle, who enjoyed his celebratory drinking, insisted on me downing a shot of whiskey before we set off for the church. I didn't like the taste at all and it didn't really mix well in my stomach with the coco pops I'd eaten for breakfast.

Uncle John was also the wedding photographer as Tony was reluctant to waste money on something as frivolous as pictures. He took some photos of me in the lounge room before we left for the church. I look at them now and see such an innocent, child virgin bride and wonder what on earth I was thinking.

It was quiet drive to the church. Once we all arrived, there were a few hurried photos before we entered the church for the long mass ceremony. In order for our marriage to be richly blessed Tony had decided that our wedding would be celebrated with High Mass which included all the bells and whistles that Catholicism provided. Once that long ceremony was over, we had more photos outside followed by a simple reception in the hall next to the church. When this reception was finished Tony told me to go sit in the car and wait for him, so eager to get the marriage off on the right foot, I obeyed. It seemed an awfully long time before he finally joined me and when he did, I asked him what he had been doing.

"I was talking to your parents and making sure they understood that I'm the head of the house now. So, they need to let me know before they come to visit. I also told them that when the babies arrive, they aren't allowed to buy just any presents for them, we will give them a list of what we need for the children. Nothing frivolous, only practical presents." Although a bit taken aback, I *had* just taken vows to "love, honour and obey", so I thought he was acting in my best interests and kept quiet. It seemed that now he had dealt with the business end he was eager to get to his mother's house for the Slovenian get together with "real food."

As soon as we had begun planning the wedding, Tony had asked his mother to hold a "real" reception back at the house for his side of the family. He didn't like Australian food, much preferring his mother's cooking. After this second reception finished, we changed out of our wedding clothes and set off for a budget hotel a short distance away.

I was a bit nervous about this first night together as I'd never shared a bed with a man before, I had no expectations or sexual desires or even been naked with anyone. I was a virgin, armed only with the knowledge of sex that Mum had told me at 12, which was sketchy at best. Despite his age, Tony also was a virgin, at least as far as I knew. It had never, ever occurred to me to ask otherwise. He had made the decision a few months before our wedding that we weren't going to have sex on that first night. Whilst in the seminary he had read about an ancient custom of offering the first wedding night to St. Joseph in order to gain the special grace of staying faithful in the marriage. According to this tradition it was also the secret to a long, blessed marriage.

There was nothing remarkable or romantic about that first night at all. Tony didn't act any differently than any other night when he'd wished me goodnight. I presumed we would have sex in the morning, but it was a very clumsy attempt on his part. He made no move to ensure I was comfortable or "warmed up", in fact it hurt so much the marriage wasn't consummated for another five months. During that time, I worried constantly that there was something wrong with me and tried to educate myself about sex from various magazines because I was just too mortified to talk to anyone about it. I felt like I was abnormal. It certainly didn't help that my mother would loudly ask me at church on Sundays, "Are you pregnant yet, Claire?"

Tony hadn't shown any interest in taking time off to go for a honeymoon, he saw it as a complete waste of time when he could be earning money at work. However, his workmates pressured him to take at least a week break, so we spent that time just driving around central Victoria, staying at cheap hotels and visiting a few tourist places. I have no special memories from this time. I only remember Tony's impatience at being pressured into taking this time off to please me and his workmates, and his constant complaints about how bored he was.

Chapter 14 – Friday

It had been an exhausting week.

With Margie's help, I'd been out inspecting houses and applying for them every single day. My head was spinning from the number of houses I'd looked at and we'd not yet gotten a reply about whether I was successful in getting any of them. I felt a huge weight on my shoulders, but I refused to give up hope.

I kept my mind occupied by staying busy and every so often I sent a prayer up to God, asking that we have a house by Wednesday. Our escape was so close and I didn't want it to fall through at the last minute.

Each afternoon when the kids got back from school, we worked to sort and pack everything. It felt really satisfying to see the rising pile of packed boxes because it made the move a reality. On my trips into Nowra, I'd been able to drop off loads of excess clothes at the charity shop.

As I'd hauled the excess away and the piles of things dwindled, I almost couldn't believe how much junk we'd actually managed to store inside the house.

Tony was due back that night and none of us were looking forward to it. We'd enjoyed our week of sorting, packing and throwing out junk, in peace, and we all knew he'd throw a spanner in the works, somehow, once he was back.

I'd noticed during the previous months that when Tony was away, the kids and I were *so* much more relaxed, chatty and happy. Although we still kept up the prayers at home and school routine, we all felt like a weight was lifted when Tony wasn't around. He was such a mood dampener. Every time he returned home, we instinctively knew that we had to "toe the line" in order to keep the peace.

That night, Tony arrived home after dark. As usual, he didn't greet us, he simply went straight to his office, set up his laptop, and for the rest of the night he sat there gambling.

Chapter 15 – Off to a Shaky Start

Once back from our honeymoon, I expected to have Tony's assistance in doing our first grocery shop together and setting up our little house. Tony reluctantly came along with me, but in all honesty, he couldn't have cared less and only complained about how much money we were spending. I didn't even have my own bank account at this time because Tony had set up a joint business account, but he handled all the finances. Occasionally he needed my signature, but I never had a card of my own or drew money out of an ATM for the entirety of our marriage. Each week he would give me a cash amount that he deemed acceptable for groceries. He even signed for and took the money from my tax return on the business account.

Our new home was a small, cheap shack on half an acre in Kinglake, north east of Melbourne, that Tony had bought a couple of years before. It had always been his dream to live in the hills, be self-sufficient and do things his way without neighbours or anyone else to answer to. The shack was very small and needed lots of work to be done on it. After spending most of my life on a farm it wasn't my ideal location, and once I'd moved to the city, I'd fast become more of a suburbs girl. But I decided to make the best of it and hoped to spend the weekends together doing it up and gardening, but that wasn't to be. Tony always made the excuse he had to work on Saturdays because we needed the money. Sundays were spent at church then the week was over; each week running into the next like Groundhog Day. He didn't seem excited to spend time with me at all, when he came home he just wanted to spend time alone.

Our first Christmas is memorable for all the wrong reasons. I was hoping for a lovely romantic festive season, but the reality was vastly different. Right from the outset, Tony insisted that Advent be kept correctly, no sex, fasting, smaller meals and no going out. The Christmas tree wasn't allowed to be put up till Christmas Eve because "it isn't Christmas till Jesus is born at midnight." He was extremely difficult to buy for as he wasn't interested in clothes, books, experiences or anything that most men wanted. In short, he had zero interest in any presents at all. His view was that it was Jesus' birthday and we shouldn't be buying presents for each other. He was also too lazy to put any thought into buying presents for anyone else and thought that if presents had to be bought then they should be practical. I struggled to hide my disappointment when I opened up my gifts: a breadboard (because we needed one) and a second-hand framed landscape print (bought from a garage sale to decorate our little house). If I would have known it then I would have considered myself lucky, I did not receive Christmas or birthday presents (unless I organised them myself) for the next seventeen years.

I was cleaning houses at this time and, in order to save fuel, we travelled to and from work together leaving at 6am. It was a long day for me because my work day was broken up with long breaks in-between. After I finished at 3:30pm, I'd travel to his work where I had to wait around till he was done at 5:30. It was half an hour travel home, then the fire had to be lit to heat water for showers whilst I cooked dinner then it was bedtime. These were very long and boring days. Tony would have been quite happy to continue living up on the mountain except that I had a car accident on the steep, windy road which made him think it was safer to move half an hour down to the small town of Whittlesea. He reluctantly put the shack up for sale and we rented a much newer unit in Whittlesea. I was much happier here because I was closer to the town, civilisation and, ultimately, the city. It had electricity connected too so there was no need to light a burner to heat water.

Not long after we moved I pestered Tony for us to go away

somewhere for an upcoming long weekend. I so wanted to be like other couples who would take off for short romantic breaks. It took a few weeks before he begrudgingly agreed, so we took the overnight train to Adelaide. I had suggested booking accommodation beforehand, but Tony refused and assured me he could get it cheaper once we arrived. We hired a car and then proceeded to waste an entire day looking for accommodation. He visited each and every motel in Adelaide asking for a cheap room. Tony wasn't willing to pay for anything decent, the last bed left in the city was a single bed in a tiny dirty room with no shower that I refused to sleep in. He drove further out into the countryside. It was getting darker and darker, Tony had stopped at every single farm house that was lit up, asking for bed.

Finally, about 9pm we stopped at the house of a lovely couple who felt sorry for us and gave us their bed for the night, asking for nothing in return. Tony was happy because he didn't have to pay for anything for the one night we stayed in South Australia, but I was beyond embarrassed and annoyed. We'd wasted a whole day just because he refused to book ahead. This was to become his hallmark whenever we went out for dates, too.

Chapter 16 – Saturday

I don't know whether Scottie had had a word with Tony and told him plainly that there was no miracle happening and we'd have to move but on Saturday morning, he actually began looking in the paper for houses to rent. I was suspicious because there was always an ulterior motive to him "helping" and I soon found out why. Tony began showing me advertisements for small 3-bedroom, 1-bathroom houses right out the other side of Nowra, in a low social economic area, albeit cheap rent.

"No way," I told him, "how are the kids going to get to school?" There was no way in hell I was going to have us living in squashed quarters again. No. I saw this move as the opportunity I'd literally waited years for, to actually get out of this cult, leave it all behind us and start fresh. Even if this wasn't what Tony wanted, the kids and I wanted it. Not only wanted it but deserved it. Tony went silent. He was angry because I didn't agree with him and I'd done the most awful thing in his eyes....I'd taken charge. He'd always told me "real women don't take charge, they quietly follow their husbands." Well I'd done the submissive thing and it didn't get me anywhere so now I was going to do what I could to make a better life for my children and myself.

I told Tony that we needed to empty the steel 44-gallon drums that were full of grain. A few years earlier, he'd decided that it would be a good idea to store various grains in large drums so that we'd at least have bread to eat, if nothing else. He had bought 10 drums and filled them with corn, barley, rye and wheat. A few times a week I would grind a variety of these grains and make fresh bread for us. I actually found bread making to be very therapeutic, especially when I was stressed or worried about something. My mind had always been too busy to meditate, mum on the other hand seemed to be able to kneel for hours with her mind elsewhere. When I was told to "meditate on the mysteries of the Rosary", I really only mindlessly uttered the words. Yet I could be totally lost in thought whilst kneading bread. Then of course there was the eating of it! The delicious fragrance of baking bread permeated the house so by the time it came out of the oven, everyone was eager for a slice. It was barely cool enough before I cut thick slices, spread butter and topped that with raw honey. Best comfort food ever!

Now that Tony had to actually throw so much grain away, brought home to him that we were indeed moving. Facing reality was never his forte, he preferred to live in his own fantasy land and anyone who dared to challenge that, was ignored. There was no ignoring that we were being evicted though and he felt powerless because everything was out of his hands now.

Chapter 17 – Baby Makes Three...Four...Five...

Tony was always on the lookout to make more money and so we came to be invited to someone's house for an information night regarding a business. I remember very clearly Tony instructing me in the car on the way there that as I had no worldly experience I was to keep quiet and not ask questions. We arrived, and I did as I was told, only exchanging formalities when required. I felt awkward, inexperienced and out of place. The meeting turned out to be a sales pitch for Amway and once Tony discovered the purpose we left.

Shortly after attending this meeting, I became pregnant with my first baby. I was very happy and relieved to finally be pregnant because, as a Catholic, this showed I was both "blessed" and "functional." I now also felt like I was real grown up woman.

I was four months pregnant for our second Christmas.

As Tony's work was closed for a couple of weeks and we'd received an invitation to visit some church friends in Sydney, we set off on a road trip. I had assumed that we would be staying in cheap motels along the way. I should have known that Tony would view this as a waste of money. There was no opportunity to take our time and enjoy the views along the way either because Tony was in a rush to get to Sydney and then back home. We made one overnight stay along the way to Sydney sleeping in the back of his 1960's Ford Ute underneath the tarpaulin cover. He didn't even ensure that we were safe, he just pulled into a darkened street and we crawled underneath the tarpaulin. It was very claustrophobic, and I didn't sleep well because not only was it quite hard and uncomfortable, but I was also scared that someone would come along. It was certainly no place for a pregnant woman.

Tony wanted me to keep working as long as possible which I did until about I was seven months pregnant. I actually preferred to be home, but quickly realised he didn't want life to change because he liked things to be the same (read: old fashioned). He constantly reminded me how European women worked in the fields, doing hard physical labour, for the entirety of their pregnancies and even went back straight after birth. He never even wanted me to visit the doctor once I was pregnant, and actually supported his position by arguing that, "Women in the olden days gave birth without much trouble, you don't need doctors. Besides, they interfere with nature too much." I was scared though because I was facing the unknown. I quietly insisted on visiting the doctor which was just as well as I developed quite severe pre-eclampsia in the last few months and required much rest. The symptoms worsened enough for me to be induced. I fully expected Tony to be there to support me during labour, but it took many months of convincing before he reluctantly agreed to be there. In the end, he was pretty much useless as he spent most of the time in the waiting room, content to watch mindless television whilst the nurses set me up with the drip. He came in at intervals to check on me, but when the nurses suggested to Tony that he come sit beside me and be supportive through the contractions, his response was "You're the nurse, it's your job." So, I spent most of my labour alone and in pain. I was so happy to finally hold my little newborn son when he arrived though!

Once home my days were very busy between being a new mother and housewife. I didn't get out much because I was quite shy and we only had the one car. Tony and I would travel down to Hampton for Mass each Sunday, the same church I had attended for almost a decade. I was feeling settled and everything was in a routine until one day Tony shattered my secure little bubble. He mentioned to me that he'd been re- reading the messages from the Virgin Mary through a seer in Bayside, NY. I'd seen these books in his cupboard at his mother's before we got married and was going to throw them out but he insisted on keeping them. In these "messages" the Virgin Mary encouraged the old-fashioned Catholics not to desert their local parishes but to be "the salt of the earth my children and set a good example to my other wayward children. Show them the way back to me and my Son."

The Bayside messages were the product of Veronica Lueken, a Roman Catholic housewife in Bayside, New York, who claimed she had experienced apparitions of the Virgin Mary, Jesus and various saints. Lueken began typing up and circulating her messages, which opposed the changes made by the Second Vatican Council regarding the deaconate, order of the Mass, and distribution of communion by lay ministers. Many of her messages had apocalyptic content with prophesies not yet fulfilled. By 1986, the Bishop of the Roman Catholic Dioceses of Brooklyn declared that Lueken's visions were inauthentic and, according to the standards set forth by the Catholic Church, her messages ran counter to the Church's teachings. This did not prevent those who were already invested in the Tridentine Mass from rejecting the messages. In fact, it drew people like Tony closer to the prophesies as they searched for security in their faith.

Without any discussion with me, Tony decided one Sunday that we would be going to Mass in the local parish instead of Hampton. This made me instantly anxious as this was really pushing boundaries into the unknown. I'd been four-years- old when I'd last attended a normal local parish and besides not remembering what it was like I didn't know what to expect. I was safe in my cocoon of going to Mass at Hampton where all the parishioners knew each other, did the same thing, and all had the same beliefs. It had been drummed into me since I was little that all these other Catholics that weren't choosing to attend the Latin Mass, even though they were well meaning, were going to hell. Tony assured me he'd help me adjust, but it wasn't quite the support I was expecting. I realised he wanted me to be just like him. He wanted me to join him in stubbornly standing up against Modernism, arrogantly informing priests they were doing the wrong thing and quoting Papal Bulls, encyclicals, Canon Law and Pastoral Theology to them. I didn't like hearing him telling the priests off in his overbearing, know-it-all attitude and felt embarrassed when he did so. He just wanted to be right and expected the priests to do what *he* deemed was the right thing to do, even though he was misinformed and judgmental. We always sat at the back of the church, me with a large scarf over my head and went to Holy Communion last so we could make a show of kneeling down and receiving the host on the tongue, which was the ancient way of receiving communion. Showing Jesus "true respect," thereby making up for the sins of others. I felt confused, embarrassed and uncomfortable that we stuck out amongst the congregation, and I could feel people staring at me. When I mentioned this to Tony, his response was always the same, "Just ignore everyone else and get used to it. We're right and they are wrong." Of course, once we stopped attending Mass at Hampton, the congregation wondered where we'd gone and began phoning up asking where we were and why we weren't going to Mass at Hampton anymore. These were uncomfortable questions that I had no idea how to answer. I honestly thought I was being a good obedient wife by following my husband's wishes.

About the same time that we moved parishes and my baby was five-months-old, I became pregnant again. I'd heard somewhere that my body would take a long time to get over the shock of labour, so I'd not thought about taking any precautions. Artificial contraception was forbidden, and I didn't really understand the natural method, so here was another baby on the way. The little unit we currently lived in only had two bedrooms, so Tony decided that we should move to something bigger.

Tony's mother had been insisting that we buy a house ever since we sold the Whittlesea shack, but Tony just didn't want any risk.

After reading the Bayside messages, Tony believed in living cheaply as possible and saving as much money as he could in order to buy gold and silver. The Virgin Mary had advised that paper money would become completely worthless towards the end of the world and one would only be able to trade in precious metals. Once the End of the World arrived and the stock market crashed, everyone and everything would be in complete turmoil. Tony's plan was then to swoop in with his gold and silver and buy the house of our dreams for a song, so to speak. To this end, Tony would save up a few thousand dollars and every few months we'd go into the city to buy gold and silver 1kg ingots.

When I think about this now it sounds utterly ridiculous, but that was before I understood the world outside of my husband's control. After we amassed a few ingots, Tony then decided that we'd need to buy coins so as not be noticed as much in the Last Days. He then began to trawl pawn shops in order to find old coins that contained precious metals. Finding this increasingly difficult he decided to buy the American Gold Eagle and Canadian Maple gold and silver 1oz coins. I remember the salesman at Deak International in the city thought it all a little weird and asked questions, which Tony either evaded or ignored. The man was obviously making a commission out of it, so he was happy to fill the order. Remembering the whole process now just makes me cringe. All this End of World talk made me feel terribly anxious, and my life was continuing to be curtailed by fear and anxiety.

We found another unit not far down the road in the little town of Whittlesea. Although larger, it wasn't as modern and light as the old one so it didn't make my soul entirely happy. The rent was cheap and that was all that mattered to Tony and since he was the breadwinner, it was more his choice than mine. My mother-in-law wasn't keen on us renting again, but Tony insisted he wasn't ready to buy yet. He was still waiting for updated heavenly messages before making his decision.

The first year passed quickly, and by the time Josh reached his first birthday, I was excited about celebrating this important milestone. I didn't have a huge party in mind, just a family celebration with a special meal and a cake. Tony shocked me by announcing he didn't want this to happen because according to him back in the "old country" Slovenia, birthdays weren't celebrated but the child's name day instead. Hence the reason for naming babies after a saint. According to him celebrating one's birthday was a modern idea and the children needed to learn from very early on that their true home was heaven, not earth. I didn't agree with this view at all. I didn't want my children forever feeling different from everyone else. I knew first-hand how embarrassing that was. Eventually they would be going to school, so they'd be attending other children's birthday parties and then to not have one of their own? I decided to take matters in my own hands and have a birthday celebration anyway. We celebrated with Tony's family, which was probably the only reason he let the birthday celebration slide. I cooked a special dinner and made a huge birthday cake and felt happy that my baby was healthy and loved.

My days fell into the usual routine of looking after my baby, still not getting out much, other than shopping and regular doctor's visits.

Apart from the morning sickness my pregnancy was easier than the first and my tiny, gorgeous eldest daughter arrived eight days early. The nurses were quite concerned because she wasn't holding her own heat very well so they literally bundled her up in a couple of big blankets, so only her tiny little face was visible. And as I held her, she looked up at me with *the* most gorgeous, big blue eyes! Even now as she's grown up, every time we meet up after not seeing each other for a while, I distinctly remember her in those first moments after she was born. Being so small, she needed feeding every few hours, so my days were very full looking after the two small children.

I'm not sure how or why Tony got it into his head to foster children, but he did and went forth with beginning the process without talking it through with me at all. I honestly had no clue what it entailed, even when the lady came to our home to interview us. I wasn't really listening to the conversation until the lady asked was if either of us had a criminal record. I knew I'd never done anything to break the law and was completely taken aback when Tony revealed that he'd spent a night in a detention centre when he was 15. He'd never told me this! He glossed over the details when answering the lady's questions, even joking around a bit. Later on, when I asked him for more details as to why he'd never told me that important piece of information before, he answered that he forgotten. I was to discover over the course of the following years that his excuse would always be "I forgot" or "I don't remember my past" in order to evade further questions or even avoid any conversation at all.

When I insisted he tell me, he eventually revealed that he'd been with a group of boys from school who were breaking into houses to look for guns. They'd just broken into a local house when they heard police sirens. A neighbour had seen the group of boys and suspecting they were up to no good, called the authorities. Upon hearing the approaching sirens, the group ran helter-skelter everywhere but unfortunately Tony got caught. The police took him to a youth detention centre where he spent the night, his father arrived the next day to get him and was very angry. In European families, it's all about "keeping face," no one must know about the unhappy marriages or family problems, keep up the happy smiling face for the public. Not unlike the Royal Family really. So, Tony's father took him home and kicked the living daylights out of him for shaming the family.

Meanwhile the lady assured Tony that as the incident had happened before he was 18, it wouldn't show up on a police check. I don't know how far the initial application went before I discovered I was pregnant with my third child. Elisa was only three months old and I had been practicing the Billings Method (a method that involves observing vaginal mucous to determine fertility periods), which was the only contraception allowed by the Catholic Church. Clearly, I'd read my cycle all wrong because I was expecting another baby.

Although I wasn't sure how I was going to manage with three children so close together, it turned out to be a blessing in disguise as the social services/foster care people decided we'd have too many of our own children; therefore, wouldn't be able to foster any children. I have to say I was relieved it didn't go any further.

Eventually Tony's procrastination about buying a house annoyed his mother so much that she decided to give him his inheritance early, so he could use it as a down payment for a house. I wasn't included in the plans. Instead, Tony and his mother talked together one day on his way home from work and he told me about it when he came home. I never said anything at the time, but I felt very left out, which led to me to feel like I had to take a back seat when it came to looking for a house.

Although we could now afford a reasonably nice house, Tony was still in the mindset of not buying anything too expensive. He argued that if we bought something that was a little run down, we could get it cheaper. My mother-in-law wanted us to live closer to her, so she could see the more of her grandchildren, so we looked at houses in the suburbs close to her. I was excited about living in the suburbs because I liked being close to people and wanted to explore the world around me and get to know other mothers when the kids went to school. Eventually we found a large weatherboard house in the suburb next to my mother-in-law. It was a large roomy house that only needed a fresh coat of paint and a woman's touch to transform it into a home. We moved in when I was about six months pregnant with my third child. I was much happier here and enjoyed putting my own special touches on the house.

After we moved in I discovered Tony had liked this particular house for reasons of his own. It occupied quite a large block of land and the front of the house was quite high off the ground. Tony decided it was the perfect place to build a wine cellar, so he enlisted the help of his workmates and they dug a large hole underneath the house. He lined it with bricks and made a big steel door to keep the heat out. His plan was that if he couldn't live in the country, then he'd bring the country to town. He had felt pressured by his mother to buy a house close to her, but given the choice he would have bought somewhere remote because he believed it would be safer in the country. Tony also paid a local carpenter to line a large cupboard near the kitchen with shelving so that we could store as much food as possible for the End Times. For those who are not familiar with End Times, this is a belief held by many world religions. For Christians, which Catholics are, the end time is seen as a period of tribulation that precedes the second coming of Christ. During the second coming, Christ will face the Antichrist and his followers and usher in the Kingdom of God. The belief is that war, conflict and famine would cover the earth, and that God's holy people (ostensibly, Catholics) would survive the hardship if they were prepared.

I thought both ideas were ridiculous but figured I could put up with this easily enough as long as we lived in the suburbs. Tony also bought a couple of guns and hid them on a friend's property in Gippsland. I didn't feel comfortable about Tony having guns in his possession or hiding them, but at least they weren't anywhere near us. He told me that once world events indicated the End was near, he would travel down and get the guns, so he'd be able to protect us and our property. Heavenly messages Tony had read said that there was going to be an influx of Asians who were going to join forces to create a big army and take over Australia. There would be street riots, those living in the cities would be forced to stay indoors and if they refused to comply to the rules, then electricity, water and food would be cut off. Hearing Tony describe in vivid detail what was supposed to happen when these Asian armies took over, scared me, made me feel anxious. He liked to watch the news on television and often commented that this or that was the "beginning of the end."

My second son arrived during the beginning of the 1992 Barcelona Olympics and why do I remember that so well?

Because once again Tony spent most of the time watching the swimming events whilst I was in labour on my own -- again. I had arranged for Josh's godmother to come mind my other children, so I could spend at least a few days in hospital recovering. My plan was dashed when Tony came to visit me the next day and told me I had to come home so that I could look after everyone. I told him that the whole reason I'd arranged for Mrs. Rayner to mind the children was so that I could have a rest. He insisted that I come home the next day, so I complied. Life was very busy being mother to three little children so close in age. It was hard to believe that my eldest child not yet even two and a half years old. Fortunately, Jakob was a quiet, well behaved baby and slept four hours between feeds and all through the night by the time he was only a month old.

For a while, things seemed to be a little better with the marriage. Tony appeared to like working together on little improvements around the house and gardening on Saturday afternoons when he wasn't working. I never brought up the Virgin Mary messages, hoping that if I dropped the subject, he would forget about it. Whilst I was boxing everything up for the move to the house we currently occupied, I'd actually mentioned that he no longer had any need for those books and that we should throw them out, but he got angry and told me to leave them alone. It was only a couple of years after we'd moved (when I thought we were lovely and settled) that I discovered he was secretly looking for somewhere else to live.

By the time Jakob was six months old, life had again settled into a routine until one weekend, in February 1993, when I felt quite nauseous. Tony and I had actually planned a rare outing at the markets on Saturday morning, so we set off. This was momentous for another reason, it was the first time ever in my life I'd had the confidence to bargain for something. I was really taken with a vase I saw and boldly bargained down the price and was very proud of myself! As the day wore on though, I felt more and more ill, eventually not being able to hold down any water or food. When we got home, I put myself to bed which was a rarity in itself. Tony sat himself in front of the TV with his new gambling program whilst I was in the bedroom becoming more ill as the night wore on. As I'd heard that ginger ale settled sick stomachs I asked him to go get some, but I couldn't even keep that down. Sunday dawned, and I couldn't go to Mass either, so he went on his own. I spent another night growing more ill, eventually calling the doctor early Monday morning. He tried to tell me it was morning sickness, but I knew it wasn't. A negative pregnancy test proved I was correct so there was only one other option; my appendix. Tony wasn't happy that his working day would be interrupted, so he took me to the hospital on his way to work. I was in so much pain that I needed a wheelchair to take me to pre-op. The operating staff all assured me it was a simple 20-minute operation and as I'd heard this often from my mother, I wasn't afraid. All too soon I was under the antiesthetic and awoke in recovery feeling very groggy, tubes coming out of me everywhere.

As I opened my eyes, I saw a blurry figure of a nurse leaning over me, "You're a very sick girl, but also very lucky, you almost lost part of your bowel." I later learnt that my appendix was larger than normal and had ruptured. I spent the next five days in hospital hooked up to a drip. Tony came past the hospital on his way home from work for a brief visit, but it was like he felt like it was an obligation to come see me. He just sat there, saying nothing. I was still so groggy. All he was worried about was when was I going to come home to look after the kids as he "couldn't," (more like wouldn't) take time off work to look after them. He was told by nursing staff that I wouldn't be able to lift anything for at least six weeks and that the local council had a program whereby you could arrange a lady to come help you for a small sum of money. Tony wanted everything for free and deemed it a waste of money. Besides he always thought that the medical staff exaggerated the seriousness of every situation. So that idea was ditched in favour of getting a lady from the parish, for free, to help me out with the washing and everyday chores. I felt terrible that Tony wasn't paying her anything so after a few days, I assured her I was fine and did everything myself.

#

In late 1993, I fell pregnant again and all seemed to be going well for the first six months, I'd put on a small amount of weight, but was still very little in size. On a routine visit at 30 weeks the doctor asked if I was feeling strong movements yet. I'd felt movements, but only very, very light ones and I was losing weight, not a good sign. He sent me for some tests which showed everything to be normal. He sent me for an ECG in the local maternity ward only a few kilometres down the road. The midwives were busy when I first arrived, so they directed me to an empty room to sit on the bed and wait for them. It was rare that I got some quiet time to myself, so I was quite happy to sit there and enjoy the view of the gorgeous autumn trees out in the garden. I was lost in the beauty of the sight when suddenly a gust of wind blew autumn leaves onto the ground. I clearly heard a voice in my head say, "Autumn leaves will cover your baby's grave." I shook my head and looked around to see an empty room. I thought to myself, *What a ridiculous thing to think. Of course, my baby will be fine.* I shrugged it off and thought no more of it. The nurses came in at that point and did my ECG which turned out normal. At my doctor visit the next fortnight he wanted me to have an ultrasound, which I arranged for at the hospital down the road the next evening when Tony came home from work.

The day dawned as normal, but then mid-morning I had some mild pain. I wasn't concerned because baby wasn't due for another five weeks; however, I made good use of my time by doing a complete house clean "just in case." By mid-afternoon I was having mild contractions, which had strengthened by the time Tony came home around 5:30. I drove myself to the ultrasound appointment, and by this time the contractions were coming every five minutes or so. Fortunately, the hospital was close and the contractions timed perfectly with the red traffic lights. I continued to have contractions during the procedure and saw a concerned look on the sonographer's face. I asked her if everything was alright.

"It's ok. I'll send these on to the hospital now for you," she said. "But

I suggest you go straight up to labour ward."

My gut told me that everything *wasn't* right, but I knew she wasn't allowed to tell me. My contractions had now worsened so I knew I needed to go to the hospital as quickly as possible. The staff asked if I was ok to drive home and I assured them I was. (How else was I going to get the car home?) Bloody amazing how the lights, once again, happened to turn red every time a contraction came on. Upon arriving home, I informed Tony that we needed to go to the hospital immediately. He arranged for his mother to come mind the kids and we set off.

The staff had already seen the ultrasound pictures and phoned the doctor. They set up an ECG monitor, every time I had a contraction, I noticed the baby's heartbeat slowed right down to 40-beats-per minute. Deep in my gut I knew something was dreadfully wrong. The doctor arrived and after examining me, informed me that I had no ammonic fluid then told me as gently as possible that my baby wouldn't survive. I refused to believe him. I'd already decided that if this baby was a girl, I'd name her Rita, after the saint of the impossible. This baby would survive against the odds and I confidently told the doctor so. He looked at me but said nothing.

A short time later tiny little Rita was born; she was blue and struggling to breathe. They asked me if I wanted a quick cuddle and I did but didn't realise at the time that would be the last opportunity to hold her whilst she was alive. I quickly handed her back, so the nurses could look after her. A few minutes later the midwives told me that they'd called the Neonatal ambulance to take her into the Royal Children's hospital and that there wasn't much chance she'd survive. They did ask if I wanted to go in with her, but Tony rudely interrupted and told them that I needed to rest so they took me to my room. About an hour later the ambulance arrived with a humidicrib. They put Rita inside and stabilised her as best they could. I honestly didn't realise how very sick she was and staunchly believed that God would heal her through a miracle.

Although I was supposed to be resting in my room, my mind was full of tumbling thoughts and wild emotions. Tony was with me, but, as usual, wasn't being any support. Not long before midnight the paramedics pushed Rita up the hallway past my door and as they walked by I again heard that same voice, "This is the last time you'll see your baby alive." I shrugged off the warning, but it proved to be very true. The nurses, obviously realising how very sick my little girl was, offered to have Tony stay the night, which he did. I didn't sleep much due to the nurses coming in to check me and also taking blood for Rita. One nurse who took my blood during the night mentioned to me again that Rita was very sick and that we should go in to be with her. Tony angrily told her I needed to rest and to leave us alone. I was terribly embarrassed and actually wanted to go into the Royal Children's to be with my daughter but was afraid of speaking up for fear of making him even more angry, so I stayed quiet. In the morning, Tony left to go home.

The nurses kept asking me if I was going in to be with Rita. Early in the afternoon Tony came by with Josh to get me and we went into the Royal Children's. I was looking forward to seeing and holding my baby. We made our way up to the critical ward where there were other sick babies. When we arrived, a nurse met us and informed us that Rita had passed away only moments before. I couldn't believe it. Surely it wasn't true? I felt numb. They showed us to this tiny, windowless, claustrophobic room and told us they'd unhook her from the machine and bring her to us. I was shocked, stunned, numb, disbelieving. What do they mean "dead"? She was supposed to survive anything because I'd named her after a saint of the impossible. I'd had faith and prayed that God would heal her. A few minutes later they gently placed a tiny, blanketed bundle in my arms, along with a tissue.

"This is to wipe away any fluids that sometimes come out of their nose or mouth after they have passed," she said quietly.

The door closed, and we were left alone. I'd never dealt with death so close before, and I was completely unprepared. I looked down at this tiny bundle in my arms. My baby. Tears and emotions overwhelmed me. I had so many thoughts, feelings and questions that I just couldn't express. I was totally at sea and felt dreadfully alone. I was aware that Tony had a few tears, but foremost in his mind was the fact that Rita had been baptised and now her soul was in heaven. He had never been good at confronting difficult situations and just wanted to go home. I didn't care about whether she was baptised or not. If I had my time back again there would be so many things I'd tell my beautiful little girl. She looked so perfect. There was no sign of how sick she had been. At the time, I was so overwhelmed and worried about what Tony wanted and thought that I didn't express any of my feelings or stand my ground at all. Josh became impatient and fidgety in the little room, as an almost four-year-old, he didn't understand what was going on. Although my emotions and feelings were all over the place, I did want to stay longer but sensing Tony's impatience I handed over my precious bundle and we left. I was both distraught and numb. I felt like I was in a bad dream. Adding insult to injury was the fact that I was asked about having an autopsy. I understood that they wanted to find out what was wrong with Rita, but I told them no.

Tony dropped me back at the hospital. The nurses were understanding and thoughtful, but surprised I was back so soon. One of them then mentioned that they had called Tony quite a few times that morning, telling him that Rita was dying, urging him to take me in there to spend time with her. I was shocked, he hadn't told me this. When I confronted him about this afterwards, he was annoyed. He told me he wasn't going to be told what to do, he would do it in *his* time, not everyone else's. It was a long, long emotionally draining night. I didn't want to be at the hospital, but I didn't want to go home either. I wanted to be with my baby and my other kids, too. I was devastated that Tony had prevented me from being able to spend time with Rita and say a proper goodbye. The thing that hit me the hardest, and still does, is the fact that she died alone. No person should die alone, and I'd *so* wanted my little girl to know how much I loved her. I wanted to caress her and hold her next to my heart. But I was denied all of this because of Tony's selfish thoughtlessness and his stupid belief that as long as she was baptised she would be in Heaven.

The thoughtful nurses set me up in a room by myself up the end, so I couldn't hear other babies crying. But it didn't matter whether I heard them or not, I cried anyway. It was a long, long night and even longer day. Tony came to take me home and as we left the hospital reception the lady asked, "Didn't you have a baby?" Tears welled up and rolled down my cheeks. I was glad to leave the hospital and loved seeing my kids again, but home didn't feel like it used to. I didn't know what I wanted or where I wanted to be. I just knew it was not in this house. I wanted to be with my kids all together because they were all that mattered.

Tony took charge of all the funeral arrangements because I honestly had no clue how to go about it. He insisted that she be buried at the Tyaak cemetery, which happens to be right in the middle of the cult property in Central Victoria. I didn't want this at all, but to him it was not only a cheap option, but he argued, "She'd be amongst family"....as he considered these cult people "family". Not only did I feel sick at the thought, I didn't want anything to do with this bloody group. As soon as Tony had gone home on the Thursday afternoon after Rita died, he'd rung Ted Stokes, the man in charge of Tyaak property who instantly contacted Kamm to ask questions of the "Virgin Mary", about Rita. According to the letter Tony received back, Rita was in heaven and had been taken from us for a higher reason. She would be given back to us at a later date, after the earth was renewed. To me this just added insult to injury. Never mind later, I wanted my baby now. Apart from the few tears Tony had shed at the Children's hospital, he was over her death already...."because she's in heaven and that's the most important thing." After he brought me home on Friday he went to a colleague's house to drink. It was a long weekend for me. I swung between tears and numbness, it was like being in a parallel universe, walking through mud. There was still the thought that it had all been a bad dream, I would wake up and Rita would be there. Tony went ahead and organised her funeral for Monday. We had a mass said but I specifically asked for her coffin *not* to be in the church because I felt if I saw the coffin I would lose it altogether. Ridiculous as it sounds, I just couldn't face thinking about my little girl being locked up in a coffin not being able to breathe. Some of the Tyaak cult members attended the mass and had arranged a small wake back at the compound so we made our way up there to bury my little girl. Again, I couldn't face actually seeing her placed into the cold ground, everything was just way too raw. So, I sat at one of the houses with a cult member making small talk and wishing I could be alone to cry out all the hurt. During the wake my mother in law patted my knee saying, "Never mind. Sick babies are too much trouble, better off dead." I was absolutely devastated and too shocked to speak. I couldn't eat and was so grief stricken that I haemorrhaged later that night. A few weeks later whilst talking to the hospital counsellor she asked me what I'd chosen for Rita to wear. My heartache resurfaced, no one had told me that I could actually choose clothes for her to wear. Not only was my dear little baby alone when she died, she was buried in strangers' clothes.

The following months were very difficult but having the three children were my saving grace. I was forced up out of bed to function each day because I had my darling children to attend to. The routine of looking after them helped me heal. The nights were very difficult though, each night I would go bed emotionally exhausted but didn't actually sleep. I seemed to go into this deep, never ending black hole. There is no other way to describe it. Tony's life carried on as normal, he went back to working 6 days a week and spending an increasing amount of time in front of the tv when home. We almost never discussed Rita, he wasn't interested in my thoughts or feelings, to him Rita was in heaven, let's just have another baby to replace her. But my baby couldn't and wouldn't ever be replaced, I didn't want to have sex. Even though it annoyed Tony I stubbornly insisted that we wait a full year before contemplating another baby. I'd read that grief takes a full year so I put my foot down.

Losing Rita taught me a big lesson in how people deal with death and who your real friends are. As I went about my daily routine with the kids, acquaintances and shopkeepers would excitedly ask me, "Where's your baby? What did you have?" and I'd have to explain in a very wobbly voice that my baby had died. Often, I was faced with shock and an awkward silence, then they would suddenly "have to go", whilst I was left standing there brushing tears away and holding my children's hands. I had two best friends that were so supportive of me and helped me through this most difficult time. Neither side of the families were empathetic. Tony's mother thought I'd gone "all weird, taking it all too much to heart," and couldn't understand why I wasn't able to let my other children out of my sight. I'd buried one child, the thought of possibly losing any of my other children was too much to bear. Despite me trying to explain my feelings to her and the reasons why I couldn't let the children out of my sight, she still didn't understand and complained to Tony about me. My own family weren't any help either, Mum only wanted to know if Rita was baptised or not because "that's the most important thing."

My mother in law had already planned an overseas trip before Rita died and she decided to go anyway. I couldn't believe she continued with her plans, my world had been shattered yet other people were acting like life went on as normal. This was the most difficult thing for me to accept but I learned quickly that just because your life has been shattered, doesn't mean everyone else is affected, or even cares. When Anna arrived back after a few weeks she brought presents over. Tony was eager to hear news of the "old country". I was holding a box of crystal glasses she'd brought back for us, when I overheard her tell Tony, "I told everyone you have 3 healthy children." I felt like I'd had the wind punched out of me and was going to faint. I had an overwhelming urge to drop those glasses and shatter them into a thousand pieces. But I resisted because, once again, I was thinking about everyone else and not myself.

I spent a lot of time writing out my feelings and thoughts during this time and wish I still had those writings, but they've gotten lost over time. One thing that stayed with me though is that I knew deep down that my marriage was over. I didn't have any particular direction, nor any idea who to turn to, just knowing deep inside me that the marriage was empty, done. So, I didn't do anything and as I've learned since, that's the worst possible thing to do. Life goes on regardless and you can choose to either be in the driver's seat or just be a passenger. Being a passenger means that life drags you along anyway, not necessarily in the direction you want.

Meanwhile my eldest son began his first year of school. Initially I was shy but soon made friends with three ladies whose children Josh was friends with. We met at each other's houses for coffee and the like. I loved every minute of it because I was beginning to feel normal, coming out of my shell and learning a lot from these women. It was the beginning of making a little circle of my own.

In the middle of 1995 I fell pregnant with Johanna, my fifth child. I had really wanted another baby and was excited to be pregnant again but found the mix of emotions difficult, especially after having lost Rita. I was nervous about the outcome of any tests yet really wanted to know that my baby was healthy. When it came time for me to have my 20-week ultrasound I wanted Tony to come with me for support. He had never taken any interest whatsoever in any tests, ultrasounds or doctor's visit before but I really needed the support this time and communicated this to him. As usual he was very reluctant citing he had to work. It was always work. I felt it wasn't fair, it was always about him and what he wanted, never about me. Here I was being the perfect Catholic housewife and mother, bearing his children, bringing them up and he didn't take any interest in my life at all. He reluctantly accompanied me to the ultrasound and when it showed everything to be normal said, "See? There was no need for me to come, the baby is fine."

I was hoping that Tony would be more supportive this birth round but once again I was to be sorely disappointed. Due to being rather big I needed to be induced, it was mid-week and as usual Tony was hoping it wouldn't take long. Yes, you guessed it...he needed to be at work. In fact, it seemed he'd rather be at work. He was even more heavily into gambling by this point and spent the entire duration of Johanna's labour reading the racing section of the newspaper whilst trying to place bets from the phone at the nurse's station. Although he was constantly in and out, he could never find the desk unattended which annoyed him no end. Due to hospital restrictions, he also couldn't use his mobile phone. Once again, I had no support because he was preoccupied with his gambling. He just wanted the baby to out as quickly as possible, so he could go to work and place bets from the phone there. I should have been courageous enough to tell him to leave right then and there. He didn't care about the children or myself. It was all about him.

Once I was home with my new baby, life once more settled into a routine. Albeit a busy one. Tony was still gambling every chance he got, at home and at work. The marriage had never been passionate; in fact, Tony was always indifferent and preoccupied. Sex was never enjoyable for me, but I do remember a couple of occasions when I did make a move on Tony after Johanna was born. He roughly pushed me off, ordering me not to touch him and turned his back on me. I was shocked and hurt by his reaction. I left him alone for a week and attempted again. He made it quite clear that I was being too forward and to wait till he was ready. I was even more hurt by his reaction and totally withdrew. Meanwhile he acted like it was the most normal thing in the world. My mind went overtime during the next 6 weeks, asking myself constantly if I was good enough, thin enough, pretty enough? What had I done wrong, was he having an affair? Then when we finally did have sex it was the same lack lustre effort as usual, leaving me feeling used.

Chapter 18 – Sunday

A week had passed already since I shared my good news of moving with the Berry Parishioners and now they eagerly awaited an update. After mass was finished, various members of the congregation crowded around asking me how I was getting on with finding a house. I really felt loved and cared for by these beautiful people, even if they couldn't help in a practical way, they offered valuable support and words of encouragement. Tony was still attending mass in the cult so unfortunately, he was already home when we got back. He was such a spirit dampener. I wished he was going back to Goulburn for the week but he'd now decided to stay because we had to out by Wednesday.

I felt a little lost that afternoon because I'd honestly done so much that week in looking at and applying for houses, there wasn't anything extra I could do at this point. There were no more houses up for rent. Every time I thought of Wednesday I got excited then the anxiety set in because we had nowhere to actually move to.

Cynthia had phoned on a regular basis to check in on me and see how the rental application process was going. I told her about the two-story Worrigee house. As it turned out, she knew the owner. He had originally bought it for him and his wife, but the marriage had broken up so now he was renting it. I didn't really take much notice of what she was telling me because I didn't think we'd be successful in getting it.

Chapter 19 – The Virgin Mary's Path

As we were living in the suburbs now, closer to cinemas and restaurants, I really wanted to go on regular dates. Tony wasn't that keen, always citing being tired from work, but agreed only to shut me up. I really looked forward to getting out and would sometimes make myself some new clothes for the occasion. I distinctly remember one time when I was proudly wearing a new outfit I'd made, a just above the knee skirt. Tony arrived home late on purpose and grumpy, but because the babysitter was already there, he was forced to go out. He openly berated me on my "immodest" dress and bluntly told me to change or we wouldn't be going out anywhere. I was devastated, but changed (even though I couldn't see anything wrong with my outfit) because I desperately wanted to go. My self-confidence was still very low, so I didn't feel comfortable going out on my own and leaving him with the kids (my instincts would later be proven correct when he lost one of our children).

When the time rolled around for our monthly dates Tony was never ready on time, could never decide about where to eat, wouldn't choose a restaurant or book ahead. Instead preferring to just drive around looking at places, hours later choosing the cheapest eatery just before the kitchen closed. Our meal would be hurriedly eaten with barely any conversation.

When I pressed him for a reason, he'd say, "Talking makes my throat dry." Then it would be off to the local pub for him to play the pokies while I sat in silence with a drink till he was finished. Movies were a little easier, but only because he *always* chose the movie he wanted to see. The one occasion that I chose a romantic movie, he sat sullenly beside me and proceeded to silently say rosaries on the rosary beads he carried everywhere. Afterwards, he told me it was the worst movie he'd ever seen, a waste of time and money.

It was really no wonder that I retreated more into my shell, not speaking up about what I wanted or needed.

It was amazing that Tony only seemed to have a dry throat when it came to conversing with me but not with others. Through old acquaintances, he had come across a religious group that were living in a community, called The Order of Saint Charbel, about an hour north of Melbourne. He was excited to discover that they also believed in End of World Theories [EOWT] and went to great lengths in getting to know as much as possible about the group. I couldn't describe my feelings at the time, but I did not get a good vibe about these people right from the beginning, but Tony was in-- hook, line and sinker. Not only did they believe in EOWT, but they also claimed the they had a direct line to heaven, which meant that, for the first time in history, a human could write a letter to a heavenly deity and receive an answer. This system meant that there was no more "trying to figure out God's Will" for yourself through hours of prayer, fasting and sacrifice. I was dubious of this practice and felt that it was going too far.

What if you received an answer that you didn't like or a direction you didn't want to follow? Tony loved the idea, but I hated the idea of losing what little control I had over my own life. We were warned to be very careful how our letters were worded because, depending on the wording, they could be understood in different ways and could get varying answers. The most disturbing part of this "write and response" practice was that after asking for and receiving a response, the writer *had* to follow that heavenly direction. If they didn't, there were dire consequences.

Tony couldn't get enough reading material from them. There were messages from "Our Lady" dating back to the late 1980's, information regarding the leader of this group The Little Pebble, who had apparently been chosen as the last pope. It went on and on. The Victorian group had a monthly prayer day, which Tony was eager to attend. I went along only to see what it really was about. I'd already prayed enough in my youth to last a lifetime, so I certainly wasn't keen to waste a whole Sunday saying even more.

As we travelled deeper into the bush towards this property on our first visit, I became more and more anxious. I hoped Tony wasn't getting ideas to move here because I was quite happy and settled in the suburbs. As we pulled up to the gate, I was shocked!

At first glance, I noticed a number of ugly old Army Nissan huts scattered across the dry barren property, which looked derelict, dry and dusty. The people walking about were wearing a strange brown layer of cloth with a huge white cross on it over their normal clothes. My heart sank as I took it all in.

Tony, however, was eager to meet everyone and hear what they had to say while I lingered behind with the children. We were invited into someone's house and immediately bombarded with questions about ourselves and information about the community. For me, it was overwhelming. There was *too* much information all at once, and all of the instructions and rituals had a sense of immediacy that put me on edge.

The community members talked about putting holy water into food and drink to kill any lethal germs that the Devil had put in there to kill us. The rationale behind this was that we were the "Chosen Ones" who were living according to God's Will, so we had to ensure that the Devil wouldn't want us around. Certain prayers were to be said while sprinkling the holy water in food, drink, around the house, and in the car before setting off on any journey. They'd even come up with the euphemism "The Old Bag" for the Devil since saying his name had the potential to alert him and make him want to hang around the person who'd uttered his name.

This is too much already, I thought to myself.

Then and there I wanted to leave, but Tony wouldn't hear of it. He was in his element and was energized as he listened to all the chatter and received more heavenly messages to read. The members tried to draw me in by being friendly and suggesting the most important practices to begin with, but it was already religious overkill and I knew that once we had those initial practices down pat, it would quickly escalate and consume our lives. I felt suffocated and drained just hearing this much and had no desire to learn any more. On the way home, I told Tony I didn't feel comfortable around the people, let alone the whole place, but he impatiently brushed me off and told me he had every intention of going back to the monthly prayer Sundays.

Tony's fascination of all things gambling continued to increase and he spent more and more time researching programs that promised winnings every week before finally "investing" in one. Now, instead of working all day Saturday, he would come home at lunchtime and spend all afternoon in front of the tv, studying this program, watching races and betting. Initially, I was excited that he was home because I wanted to spend time together as a family and doing things that were fun together, so I was bitterly disappointed when he abruptly brushed the kids and I aside in order to gamble. I hated his gambling and openly said so. I saw it as nothing more than a waste of money since no one ever got ahead betting on anything, and I told him so. He got very annoyed, then snapped at me before finally ignoring us all and continued gambling till late into the night.

Throughout 1995, Tony became increasingly involved in attending the prayer days at Tyaak, and I absolutely hated the place. Every time we went I visited Rita's grave and each time I left in tears. I missed my little girl terribly and it caused me great sorrow to know that I had not been allowed to spend the final hours of her short little life with her, and, worse, it made me feel totally powerless.

There were stirrings of change in my heart, but I allowed my fear of the unknown and of being a single mum keep me in my marriage. Over and over, I told Tony how much I disliked the community, and how much I dreaded the prayer days and the weirdness of its members with the hope that he would eventually see the light and let go of it, but he refused to listen to my complaints for very long and quickly shut me down. When I pursued the subject, he got very angry. He seemed to have an idealistic idea that living in a community, where everyone was devoted to helping one another, would be a breeze, and he disliked me challenging this ideal. To him, I was a dream wrecker.

The "community" at Tyaak wasn't anything like the picture he painted of the European communities of days gone by and I definitely didn't want to move there. Every time I visited there were rumours of infighting, disobedience and people not following orders. I knew it was not a place I would ever been happy in, but Tony persisted. After collecting more printed messages each prayer day, Tony would spend copious amounts of time pouring over the messages and dissecting them then follow this with hours of talking on the phone with various members. He was constantly asking for interpretations of the messages and asking whether it was safe to be living in the suburbs. He wanted to know if he should he move his family to a community or at least a country property and become more self- sufficient. I felt like he was looking for a way to destroy what little happiness I had left.

Every mention of moving made me feel anxious and talk of the end of the world made me feel physically ill. Tony tried to convince me that it was better to be informed than not because you were ahead of "the herd" in the world. It seemed to me that every "message" described progressively more terrible punishments, and I wanted none of it. I mentioned this to Tony quite often, but he chose to actively ignore me. The more I hated it, the more it seemed he involved himself and it angered me that he would quite happily spend hours talking on the phone to cult members, but then be sullen and barely speak to me. It felt like he was having an affair.

In early 1996, towards the end of my pregnancy, Tony and I met William Kamm, the leader of The Order of Saint Charbel, in person for the first time. We met with him at the Seymour community, which was a relatively new community and a little further away from Tyaak. Kamm introduced me to Josie, a lovely lady, who was very practical and down to earth. I felt a little bit of hope because she seemed like someone I could talk openly with. At the time, I silently wondered why someone so pragmatic was so heavily involved in Kamm's movement, but it soon became obvious that it was due to her grandson Beau, who had, apparently, been receiving messages. Josie and her husband, Peter, had made their small property into a mini-community adding a little chapel to the end of the house in preparation for the End of Times. They began having prayer days in addition to Tyaak and, of course, Tony was attracted to this new "home", rather than the one where his own family lived. I never put the prayer days on the calendar or even mentioned them because I hoped that he would forget. Unfortunately, he always seemed to remember. Between Seymour and Tyaak, there were now two prayer days to attend each month.

What I didn't understand until much later, was the extent to which William Kamm was a wolf in sheep's clothing (Australian investigative journalist, Graeme Webber, would spend years researching Kamm and his community and eventually publish his book *A Wolf Among the Sheep)*. His communities were founded on the premise that God had appointed him, "The Little Pebble," to serve as the last Pope before the end of the world. The Little Pebble was to establish a court of eighty-four queens and princesses, whom he would impregnate through a "spiritual embrace" and implant his seed using his "holy shining thing" so that mankind would survive after Judgement Day. The Little Pebble would be assisted by the Virgin Mary (aka "Our Lady") who would advise the community members as to who would be a queen and who would be a princess through a range of holy messages conveniently passed to the community members through none other than The Little Pebble himself.

Kamm, as he was known by the members of the various communities, liked to get around to each community, in Australia and overseas, in order to touch base and get to know the people whom "Our Lady" had chosen to be in charge of each property. If his priestly sidekick, Malcolm Broussard, was with him, then a Mass was said, but if Broussard was not present, then prayers were recited in order to bring about a special message and blessing from the Virgin Mary. Often "Our Lady" would confer special appointments to certain people (such as promising that an important seer would rise up with some unique mission for the End Days). My first reaction upon seeing Kamm was one of surprise, I'd never met a man so short and portly or as hairy.

He didn't look like someone God would have entrusted with such a holy duty. The other thing that left me confused was the way various women had gushingly told me how females threw themselves at him. I honestly couldn't see what they were on about.

Tony was very happy to at last be able to meet Kamm and took the opportunity to ask questions about possibly moving to one of the communities. Kamm only gave general answers, advising Tony to write to the Virgin Mary to find out for sure what God's Will was for our family. Tony was really excited to be able to have this "phone line to heaven" that would enable him to ask what he wanted. However, we had been warned by members of the community, on one of our visits, to be very careful in how we phrased our questions because once we'd asked the questions then we had to follow through with the directive whether we like it or not, otherwise Heaven would be displeased. This warning stemmed from the early days when Kamm's followers had found out that they could write letters to the Virgin Mary. They'd gotten quite excited and asked anything and everything but found that they weren't always happy with the answers.

When I look back and see the community from a distance, I can see how it was quite ingenious of Kamm to control his worldwide followers this way. And he would continue this practice even after he was tried for paedophilia and sentenced to time in prison.

After meeting Kamm at Seymour, Tony was more determined than ever to move from our suburban home to somewhere in the country. If there wasn't any room in a Saint Charbel community somewhere in Australia, then he was determined to find a cheap rural property that was close to a community. Tony was reluctant to buy a house again, and he saw moving to a community as a way out of paying off a mortgage or even having to pay rent. I resisted against the idea of moving any time the subject came up, especially since I was about to give birth again and the kids were nicely settled into school.

If Tony wasn't gambling, he was poring over messages trying to dissect God's Will for us. Each time we attended the prayer days he asked numerous questions to the members about moving. He had mentioned to me about writing a letter to Our Lady, but every time he brought it up I made it clear I didn't like the idea. I was deathly afraid of the answer. Eventually, he got annoyed with me because, from his perspective, I was willfully delaying God's Will for our family. So, he went ahead and wrote a letter to Kamm, who quickly responded and suggested Tony come up for a visit.

The only holiday we'd ever been on as a was after Rita had died. Tony always said we couldn't afford holidays, it was a waste of money and he was supposedly saving for our future. So, when he suddenly got all enthusiastic about going to Nowra for a holiday, I was suspicious and anxious. Not anxious that he was going away on his own but dreading the outcome of the visit.

Firstly, he did something unheard of, he actually took off the whole Melbourne Cup weekend and travelled 16 hours up to Nowra and back on very little sleep. When he returned, he described everything as "beautiful", "wonderful", "exactly where I want to bring up the family", "truly Christian people, you're going to love it." But I already knew I wouldn't. In fact, I couldn't think of anything worse than moving to some little, hick town I'd never heard of, with no decent shopping centre and going back to country living.

He enthusiastically related how happy he was that he'd gotten to actually see and speak with The Little Pebble alone. He explained how Kamm had advised him to write to Our Lady for an answer about where to move and when. As he spoke, I felt physically sick and my emotions began shutting down. My life was spiraling in a direction I didn't like, but my thinking was still very Catholic, so I felt guilted into being obedient to all directives from priests, my husband and, as crazy as this sounds, whatever Our Lady would tell us. I didn't have the life experience or skills to know that I should have listened to my intuition over and above anyone or anything else, and that, had I done that, I would have most likely found all the answers and strength necessary to steer my life in the direction *I* wanted for myself and my children. Instead I continued my everyday life, hoping against hope that Tony would listen to reason and give up this stupid idea after considering my happiness as well as his own, but Tony proceeded to write the letter to the Virgin Mary and sent it off without telling me or even showing me the contents.

A few weeks later, while Tony was at work, I collected the mail. I instantly recognised Kamm's distinctive scrawl and despite the envelope being addressed to Tony, I opened it. Inside was the answer I had been dreading. "Our Lady" had replied that, although there was currently no accommodation or housing at the main community in Nowra, we were to move there. I was shaking as I read this awful news, my heart sunk to the pit of my stomach and I felt sick to my very core as I cried silently. I decided to ring Tony to see if there was a possibility that we didn't have to actually obey this request, but he was relieved and happy to hear the answer was to his liking. When he arrived home that night, I wanted to talk at length about the whole moving house scenario, instead of him making an impulsive decision without my consent. Tony had a completely opposite reaction to the letter than I did. He believed that "Our Lady" had written her wishes and in order for us to be happy and gain a high place in heaven, we needed to cut ties with our old life and embrace a new life in this community. I was to be a good submissive wife, accept my husband's decision and everything would turn out just fine. Despite me approaching the subject of my feelings about the move in a variety of ways, Tony always managed to shut me down. For him, it wasn't just about how I felt about this or anything, I needed to be able to present valid Catholic faith-based reasons for why I felt the way I did. I had no idea of how to go about expressing my point without becoming angry, frustrated and emotional, in a way where he would hear me. In the days and weeks that followed, Tony steamed ahead in getting the house valued and putting a For Sale sign out in front of the house. Then he announced to his family that we would be selling the house and moving to Nowra. They weren't enthusiastic about it, to say the least. His mother was upset because we had bought our house only a few years prior, but they refrained from saying much because they knew how absurdly stubborn Tony could be and that no matter how strongly they objected, it was likely that he would go through with his plan anyway. One day, as I was helping him to fix his truck, I mentioned that I wasn't comfortable selling the house and moving. I explained how uncomfortable it made me that he had gone ahead and organised it all without consulting me or considering my thoughts and feelings. Tony got very angry and reiterated the fact that this was "all for the good of the family, so we will have a better life." He scolded me, saying that if only I would let go of my will and just agree with him, everything would be just fine. I was upset and angry as I walked away.

I have often wondered how different my life would have been if I'd simply destroyed the letter.

Now that he had the answer he wanted and had put the move into motion, he went ahead and arranged for us to spend a couple weeks at the community over the Christmas holidays. I was extremely resentful of this since every year since we'd been married, I had longed to go for a proper family holiday, but Tony had opposed it by saying we couldn't afford it. Now, suddenly, we could afford to spend a holiday in this desolate community?

Although, at the time, I didn't understand that Saint Charbel was a cult, in my gut, I just *knew* something was off about the place and I wanted no part of it.

The journey to the Saint Charbel community was long and hot, and we took very few breaks because Tony was so eager to get there as quickly as possible. In his mind, he felt he'd be able to relax once we arrived. His rationale was that not only had he had found what he had been searching for all these years, but also that his family would be taken care of.

A few years later, I was horrified to discover his real reason for wanting to move to the community when he told me, "I knew I couldn't be a real father to the kids, so I thought it was wise to move to a community where other men could take my place." I was shocked beyond belief. Not only that he'd decided to abdicate responsibility, but that he thought strangers would somehow fill in the gaps left by his absence.

The closer we got to the community, the further we drove into the bush and the more uneasy I felt. When we finally reached the property, we were met by the ominous site of imposing gates and a tall barbed wire fence that stretched as far as the eye could see and enclosed the perimeter of the property. Although only a few kilometres from the small local town, it felt like we were in the middle of nowhere.

The property was dry, unkempt and littered with old caravans and mobile houses. This was *not* where I'd envisioned living or bringing up my children, I loved having a house of my own, not sharing a property with others. Tony had told me that the property was actually an old caravan park on 40 acres and Kamm had kept the license going so that he could have quite a number of people live there. As Tony had visited here only a few weeks before, he parked the car and led us down towards the chapel that had a dining room underneath. I didn't see many people about since most of them were in the chapel saying prayers. The first person we met was Jan Williams, Kamm's personal secretary who guarded the office and managed all of Kamm's business. She greeted both of us in a cold, clipped manner that, over the years, never changed. No matter how faithful to Kamm the community members were, she remained suspicious and, on sight, I didn't trust her. That feeling never wavered the whole time I knew her.

Jan led us downstairs to the dining room where she informed us that all the other members would shortly gather for lunch, so we would meet them then. We were introduced to a couple of members who were doing the last-minute preparations for lunch. I felt very uncomfortable about this community idea of eating meals as one big crowd. It was noisy, claustrophobic and reminded me of religious orders, which I wanted nothing to do with. When I'd married, I'd wanted my children to experience family meals, where we each talked about our experiences during the day while everyone else listened. I wanted my children to feel like their parents listened to them. As the community members entered the dining room, my heart sank further. The clothes they wore brought back all the bad memories of my childhood, this was something I'd worked hard to erase in the years since I'd left home. Even though I was still very Catholic in my thinking when it came to clothing, and didn't wear jeans, trousers or t-shirts, I had gradually tried to modernise my outfits in order to make myself fit in a little better. These peoples' clothes were not only outdated and shoddy, they also covered them with big, ugly, mission brown scapulars that bore a massive white cross. I was informed that this scapular was only the beginning of a religious habit that all members eventually chose to wear instead of regular clothes, and to add insult to injury, *all* of the women had to wear a veil like a nun. It dawned on me that Kamm was attempting to create a religious order and Tony had duped me into giving up my freedom for something I'd never wanted.

As people filed downstairs we were introduced to Vito Napolitano, the Third Branch Superior. While he seemed friendly enough, his wife, Cathy, didn't have a great command of English and rarely mixed with anyone due to being the main caretaker for their eldest son Thomas, who had MS and was in a wheelchair. Cathy would attend Mass and prayers then go straight back home which was right across the dirt track from the chapel. Vito's role was to take charge of the married and single people in the Third Branch. In essence, he was our direct supervisor and any problems we had needed to be taken to him. It was also his responsibility to ensure all those under his direction were living according to the Rule and Constitution of the Order. I would soon learn that it was Vito who gave (or denied) permission for all trips outside the property. Although friendly enough, once living there we discovered Vito was essentially Kamm's puppet. He was a hard-working Italian and expected everyone else to follow the rules, and despite being fairly simple, there were always those who flouted the rules on a regular basis. Vito's job was to admonish them, but the rule-breakers would often go behind his back to whinge to Kamm who would excuse them from the rules. This power play was often used by women who were either one of his queens or princesses or, at the very least, on his Royal House of David list. This caused constant infighting, so at any given time we had about half the community following the rules and sharing the workload while the other half freeloaded.

Another person I met that day was Malcolm Broussard, a suspended Catholic priest from Houston, Texas, and he reminded me of William Welsh, the priest who had been found to be sexually abusing minors after spending time at my childhood home. Malcolm was mysterious and never revealed much about himself despite the fact that Tony tried to engage him in conversations about his past by asking what seminary he attended and whether he was familiar with the Tridentine mass. Malcolm always looked uncomfortable and would reply, "The Little Pebble and Our Lady have told me not to talk about my past due to people misconstruing it." I was suspicious of him right away and was determined to keep my ear to the ground to find out what he was hiding. Over the next few years we would discover that he had been suspended in 1989 by the Bishop of Houston and had hidden out in Australia while ignoring his Bishop's requests to come back and sort things out. He was therefore seen as "not in good standing" with the Catholic Church. Malcolm of course denied all these allegations, telling everyone that eventually the world would know the truth when Our Lady revealed it all in good time. Around 2003, Malcom was excommunicated by the Catholic Church after his episcopal ordination was deemed unauthorized by the Catholic Church, but since he'd been successful at hiding his past misdeeds, only Kamm was aware of this.

I felt very uncomfortable attending Mass and prayers in the chapel because I could feel the others looking me up and down the entire time. We soon discovered that everyone had a certain seat in the chapel, so we were left to find a spare one. The hierarchy of the community was evident in the fact that those members of some importance had wooden kneelers with their names on them, while everyone else sat in grey plastic chairs and knelt on the carpet. I did notice that Kamm's chair was a Bishop's Throne, (a special chair used in churches for when the Diocesan Bishop pays a visit) placed at the back of the chapel just inside the door. At this early point I also found it very strange that he was constantly surrounded by pretty young girls who would kiss him on the lips as they came and went. As the years went by I would learn that these girls were his favourites, and it seemed there was a constant jockeying for position of favorite. Almost as soon as Tony saw this he mentioned to Kamm that it didn't look very holy for him to be seen kissing young girls on the lips, but Kamm just smiled and told us it was German custom.

I was quite surprised when I met Bettina, Kamm's second, much younger wife. Talkative, spirited and happy, she was eager to meet any new women who moved to the community. She invited me over to her house to chat and I was overwhelmed by her enthusiasm for community living. Bettina showed me at least half a dozen books of questions she'd written to Our Lady over the years, and the accompanying answers. I felt really uncomfortable about all this heavenly letter writing and the supposed answers that were given. I felt I was being drawn into a spider's web with no option of escape.

As I left the chapel on one of those first occasions I noticed Cathy, Vito's wife lying on the floor of the chapel hugging a crucifix to her chest, looking like she was asleep. I was so intrigued I stared to the point of rudeness because I'd never seen anything like this before. C.C., who I later discovered was a major queen, eagerly informed me that Cathy was a seer who would go into ecstasy during every rosary or public vision that Kamm had. Apparently, she was shown various scenes of future events, good and bad that she recorded in a book at home to be verified later as true, by Kamm.

Hearing this was disturbing and made me doubt Tony's desire to move us into this community even more strongly.

Tony considered these two weeks away as bliss and enthusiastically threw himself into the community. He became animated in a way that I'd never seen before; meeting and talking with everyone that came across his path, asking lots of questions and then trying to convince me that *this* would be the best life for all of us. All of the pressure caused me to pull back and retreat into myself as I took care of my children and made the least possible effort to mix and mingle. I couldn't believe that my own husband would actually move us to a place that made me so miserable already, and I was *still* hoping against hope that all the plans Tony was making would fall through and that life would return to normal in Melbourne. Tony was very easily persuaded to only see the rosy side of this community living, and any objections that I brought up were quickly brushed aside by either Tony or other members. I was told that if I stopped being so standoffish and involved myself more then I'd see that this was indeed the life to live, we would be *so* much better off in so many ways. There would be no mortgage stress, the mothers would help and support each other, and the community would be self-sufficient, so we wouldn't need much money.

Despite all of the happy smiling faces and non-stop convincing, my nagging doubts were never far away, and, in the days that followed, I felt like I was being slowly choked to death by all the questions that were hurled at me about my life. My privacy was invaded, and it was very tempting to run, so once the car was headed towards home, I was *very* relieved.

Chapter 20 – Monday

I felt a bit down when I woke up on Monday morning. It didn't help that Tony was there too, I felt that his melancholy attitude wasn't helping anyone's situation. I tried to put on a bright and happy face for the childrens' sake because they'd already been through more than enough, and because their help had been invaluable over the past week and I didn't want them to feel like it was all for nothing.

That morning, I sent them off to school and busied myself with various things around the house. After lunch, I could feel the anxiety start to set in as my shoulders hunched from the weight of worry. I knew I had to stay positive, but it was really difficult to have the sole responsibility of securing housing for everyone, organizing the move and taking care of a thousand other things I needed to do.

Caroline, from next door, phoned for a chat. She and her family had moved from New Zealand to live in the cult and initially had been staunch supporters. However, once it became clear that Kamm was a criminal, they began making plans to move out. I updated her on our housing situation and she suggested following up the real estate with a phone call. "It can't hurt," she said. I was so scared of being rejected that it took me a while to buck up the courage to actually call. Finally, around 5pm I couldn't take the stress anymore. I needed to know one way or the other.

The receptionist answered my call and told me that the agent was busy, so she'd call back before they closed.

At that moment, everything overwhelmed me. I sat on the step in the back room with a thousand "what ifs?" flooding my brain. My head felt like it would explode from the pressure. If the answer was "no," then it would be back to the drawing board to try finding a house by the next night.

My thoughts were interrupted by the ringing of the phone.

It was the agent returning my call.

I waited breathlessly for the answer to my question. "Your application has been accepted for the Worrigee house. You just need to call the Housing Commission to organize the bond and once that's done you can sign papers tomorrow afternoon and move in," said the agent.

I exhaled a loud sigh of relief. It was almost unbelievable! I'd gotten us a house!

After the agent hung up, I took a moment to process what had happened. All of my hard work had paid off, and the stress and worry had been worth it. In less than 48 hours, we would be off this property and out of this cult for good. After spending almost a decade here, it was hard to imagine actually living somewhere else. I couldn't imagine what it would feel like not being spied on or dictated to.

I reminded myself that I didn't have time to concentrate on that right now, though.

My whole body felt light as I went to tell the kids the great news. They'd not seen the house, so I described it to them again. Seeing their excitement made me feel happy. Tony, however, was sullen and silent; refusing to share in our excitement. He didn't like the idea of living in the suburbs at all, and even though he hadn't seen the house, he didn't like the sound of it, especially as he'd had no say in applying for it. I had applied for it myself, so his name wasn't on the lease.

I finally had something that was *mine*.

Chapter 21 – Nowra

After two weeks in the community at Nowra Tony was even more determined to sell the house as quickly as possible and move. Each day that passed, he became increasingly frustrated that things weren't moving faster, and late one afternoon, I was mortified to overhear him verbally abusing the real estate agent on the phone because the agent had mentioned that wanting to sell so quickly meant he couldn't get the high price Tony was asking for the house. I'd always been taught to treat others as you want to be treated, so hearing this made me feel both embarrassed and angry. Shortly afterwards, we had a buyer who wanted a quick settlement, so the decision was out of my hands. Tony had kept the move from his family until the very last minute and I'd avoided telling my new-found school mum friends that we were moving in a hurry. One mother made a comment about it being a cult, but since I had no real understanding of what it actually meant, it went straight over my head.

The closer we got to the move date, the more I felt sick and anxious. I was happy here in Montmorency; in this house, this state, this city. I was branching out and making friends, feeling more normal than I ever had. This was the beginning of my blossoming, but now my leaves were being pruned in a way that didn't feel healthy or productive.

Tony was ecstatic that we could at last follow Our Lady's will for us and our family. He kept working and, as usual, left it to me to organise all the packing and actually get it all done. As we were now going to be living a "community life," (the very words made me sick), I had to get rid of superfluous things like pretty wine glasses and other wedding presents. It wasn't like we had much anyway, but Tony assured me we wouldn't need such "fancy" things anymore as we would be living a very plain life with few or no luxuries.

The last day of freedom arrived all too soon, and I felt sick as we packed the kids into the car, then travelled overnight and arrived at the compound in the early morning. Despite there not being an actual place for us, Kamm assured us "Our Lady" would provide, and she did. We were "provided" with a tiny mobile home on the main property that couldn't have been more than 11 square metres. It contained two very small bedrooms, a squishy kitchen and miniature bathroom, so almost all of our possessions had to be put in storage until a larger, more permanent accommodation could be found. We lived in this hut for about month while everything was up in the air, and I found it quite stressful because there was no room to escape, the humidity was oppressive and Nowra had nothing to offer by way of an escape.

During those first weeks of living there we were forced to take the dreaded vows of the order. Privately I put up a real fight against joining the order, which made Tony annoyed, then angry. Kamm had leaned on him hard about how we wouldn't be allowed to live on the property until we both joined and made it seem like I was the only head strong wife putting up a fight.

When I finally gave in, a set of ugly brown scapulars were made up for us, and that Sunday we took our vows.

My body was there but my heart was most certainly not. I mouthed the vows but didn't mean a word of them. Afterwards, I felt physically ill and teary every single time I had to put the awful scapular on. I made my feelings abundantly clear to Tony, but, as with every other time I'd expressed my feelings about anything, he wasn't interested in my views, thoughts or feelings. He brushed it off and told me, "Just go along with it, you'll get used to it." I knew I was *never* going to get used to wearing this ugly thing. When I left home, I thought I'd escaped everything having to do with a convent, but here I was, again, being forced to wear a nun's habit anyway. I was quite open in my distaste for wearing this scapular and declared that there was *no* way I would wear a habit. When other members heard my objections, they attempted to laugh it off and assure me it wasn't happening in a hurry and that we'd all have time to get used to it. I put on a happy face not only as a coping mechanism for the sake of my kids, but also to protect myself from prying eyes. However, once I was alone behind the walls of our hut, I struggled mentally and emotionally. I felt like a trapped animal, and the net was getting tighter every day. For a while, Tony was really happy and he constantly took off to meet, greet and spend time with everyone, coming back all excited about all the "lovely people" he thought I should meet. What he failed to recognize was that I did *not* want to meet these "nice" people. I didn't know them, nor did I want to know them much less trust any of them.

In an attempt to maintain my sanity and create some sense of normalcy for the children, I implemented a routine. My two eldest children began going to the school on the property, which was a big change for them. The school they'd come from was a state school that had a large number of students. The Saint Charbel school, although sanctioned by the government, was run by cult members, had only members' children as students, and used a government approved curriculum that was barely followed. The children spent most of their time in prayer and religious study, and, dreaded both by me *and* the children, the Catechism lessons included large sections that addressed Our Lady's messages. The reasoning behind this was two-fold. First, teaching children about the messages was essential to the survival of the community since they contained certain "mysteries" of the Catholic religion that enhanced students' understanding current Church teachings. A second, more sinister reason, was that some of the school children had been (or would be) chosen by Our Lady as seers. I definitely didn't want my children to attend this school, but since Tony wouldn't allow them to go anywhere else and the community backed him up, I felt like I had no choice. He reminded me over and over that we were supposed to fit in and not rock the boat, and the warning was loud and clear: put up and shut up.

During the first month that we lived in the Saint Charbel community, the members treated me as a curiosity, not only because I was new, but also because I was determined to retain the parts of myself that were more modern and so I resisted looking frumpy despite everything that the community did to ensure that I would. Before leaving Melbourne, I had bought some nice clothes since I knew that Nowra didn't have a big shopping centre. These clothes weren't high fashion by any means, but they definitely set me apart from the rest of the women who dressed in a manner that grated on me, and the fact that they eagerly embraced the idea of wearing a religious habit and were keen to share that enthusiasm with me, irritated me to no end.

The lack of privacy also rubbed me the wrong way, especially when members, mainly the young ones, would visit without notice and ask me endless questions; many of them quite personal. I wasn't used to people prying into my private business and I resented it. A large part of my resentment stemmed from the fact that my mother had been extremely inquisitive about my movements, so when I finally left home it had been a relief to be able to do things without having to report back and account for every movement all the time, and now I felt like I was right back where I started. The younger girls in the community talked a lot about Kamm's "Royal House" and asked whether I'd been chosen to be a Princess. They were so sure that I had been, but I had no knowledge of the Royal House of David, so I treated them like silly gossips and ignored most of what they said. Ironically, had I understood what they were talking about, I would have known that they let slip many of the cult's secrets, but at the time, whether through ignorance or a desire to keep myself separate from the community, it all went straight over my head.

The members were also eager to share the special history of the property. According to what Our Lady had told Kamm in numerous messages, these 40 acres had been chosen from the beginning of time specifically for a community of hers with Kamm as its head. Since he was going to be the last pope, this property would be the new Rome after the earth was cleansed by chastisements. Each community had been given a name that was particular to the group of people and the tribulations that would be sent to their community. The Nowra acreage was called Gethsemane, after the rock Jesus had leaned on during his suffering before he was crucified. I had noticed a huge rock sitting in the middle of a rectangle of concrete below the chapel and wondered about it. Various people informed me that Our Lady had given Kamm instructions that the real Gethsemane rock in the Holy Land had been swapped by angels with a fake one. The real one had been secretly flown to this chosen property by the angels and Kamm was instructed to dig it up and display it near the current chapel. Further instructions indicated that a chapel was to be built around it and thousands of worldwide pilgrims would gather to witness miracles performed through it by "special" seers who purported they could see the actual blood of Jesus speckled on the rock.

In August of 1997, the first "Mystical Baby" was born. The young mother of the mystical baby girl was only seventeen and named the first child of the New Hoy Era, Sapphire. She also claimed that she was still a virgin since the baby had been born via Caesarean. I found it to be ridiculous, but kept my mouth shut because Tony had made it clear that I'd asked one too many questions and ordered me to keep quiet. That same month, also marked the wedding of a young couple that Our Lady had preordained for marriage. The bride was engaged to a young man who had been in the cult since his teenage years. The groom had spent time in the Army reserves and, due to this experience, was chosen to be one of Kamm's bodyguards. A few years before the wedding, he and the girl had received messages from the Virgin Mary telling them that it was God's Will they should be married. The problem was that the young man was in love with one of Kamm chosen queens. This posed a serious problem since all queens were to remain legally unmarried, while "mystically" married to Kamm. The preordained wedding seemed a convenient way to eliminate the young man as a competitor for any of the queens while also bolstering the power of Our Lady's messages. It worked, and on the day of the wedding, the community packed inside the small chapel to witness the wedding and then moved on to the reception. The couple seemed happy enough, but as I watched them celebrate, I felt sad -- for them and for myself.

Meanwhile the living conditions continued to deteriorate. Despite the grounds being a caravan park, many sites remained empty and the mobile homes that littered the landscape were derelict reminders of the fact that Kamm couldn't (or wouldn't) stretch the money to buy more mobile homes. Instead, he encouraged members to buy them and fix them up themselves, but since many of them didn't have jobs or were on welfare benefits it was difficult for them to find the money necessary to make the repairs. However, while most of the community lived in crowded, dilapidated conditions, Kamm lived in the biggest house on the property with air conditioning, five televisions and many of the basic comforts that most of the rest of us lacked. Kamm's house always seemed to be undergoing renovations in order to increase some aspect of his comfort, and as I looked around the tiny trailer my family occupied, I couldn't help but resent him.

Living on the property made me feel very alone and instinctively knew I had to carefully protect myself and my kids. I missed Melbourne terribly and the big roomy house we had lived in. In fact, it took quite a few years before I stopped grieving the move and many more years before I even recognised that I resented Tony for what he'd done. There was no beauty in my immediate surroundings, our house sat in the middle of bushland, and the drab community buildings were all I could see. Once we moved to our house beside the cult property, Tony had insisted on hanging crucifixes and medals in *every* room and topped it off by creating a mini-chapel in our lounge room, complete with large angel statues. Nowra itself was very small, it had a low socio-economic population, and was unattractive with no decent shopping centre, which, in the larger scheme of things, didn't matter because we were discouraged from shopping for anything other than the bare necessities. This suited Tony perfectly since he had always felt that pretty things were unnecessary and that none of us ever needed more than a couple sets of clothes. He said that the only decorations a religious family should have in their home were statues, holy pictures, crucifixes or pictures of scenery, and if anyone objected, he would support his perspective by saying, "We are only pilgrims on this earth, our souls yearn for Heaven and that's where we should have our focus." What I didn't understand was that if my focus was on heaven, why couldn't I also enjoy what this earth had to offer whilst I was living here?

After a month of living in very tight quarters, we were told we would be moving to the back of a shop that Kamm had bought in North Nowra till a larger accommodation was organised. I was relieved to hear this news because, despite how disappointing the town was, at least I'd be amongst normal people, even if I didn't actually know them. It also meant that I would have distance from all the inquisitive people in the Saint Charbel community and it would make it much more difficult to attend all the prayers and meals. While there was a little more breathing space in these quarters, my relief was short lived. Due to the fact that the shop was staffed by community members, there seemed to be at least one person who had nothing to do and eager to socialise with me, which meant that now my days were spent in needless chatter and my carefully organized routine was destroyed. I hated it.

The house that Kamm bought belonged to a retired couple who lived on seven acres. They had initially joined what they saw as a nice community, but over the years, as rumours circulated about what Kamm was really up to, the husband refused to be involved in any community activities and began attending Mass in the local parish.

His wife steadfastly maintained her belief in Kamm and continued to attend Mass at the chapel every day. Their house had originally been built with the End Times in mind, so it was quite large, so when the husband made it clear that he wanted to distance himself from the cult, Kamm offered to buy the house and moved the Maoris in there. As soon as they had taken possession, the Maoris began telling Kamm what they wanted added or fixed, which resulted in yet another ongoing renovation project.

Everything about the physical life in Nowra was exhausting. The land was dry and desolate, the scenery was bare, the accommodations were barely livable, and my stubborn resistance to adapting to life in the community made every day a chore. However, I still felt an obligation to honour my marriage vows and make my family work for the sake of my children, so I trudged along trying to keep my head down and my mouth shut, but the cracks, which had started to show before we moved to Nowra, were beginning to widen and my patience with the community --and with Tony-- was wearing thin.

#

Shortly before we moved to the rear of the shop, Kamm set off overseas on a major tour promoting his cause before the "Warning" that was prophesied to arrive in early June.

Unbeknownst to us he'd had his eye on a property that was alongside his current one and had been up for sale for quite some time.

Although he'd put several offers in to buy it, the owners had repeatedly refused because they knew he was running a cult.

Before Kamm left, he told Tony that since we were new in town and had just sold our house in Melbourne, we should buy the property and live in it. Tony was very happy with this idea, as it meant we would be living right beside the Saint Charbel community and could still be involved in the daily routine.

Kamm also proposed that Tony farm the land there as this was the ultimate goal for the communities, so they could be self-sufficient. The problem was that the property consisted of a small patch of land that had the house and a few sheds on it. The rest of the land was very steep, rocky and bushy, which made it unfit for farming, but Tony was sure he could something with it.

The house wasn't anything to write home about either. It was dark, dingy and small, but the one positive note was that we wouldn't be actually living amongst the community members.

Without consulting me, Tony went ahead and put a deposit down on the property and had the papers, with our names on the title, drawn up. At the time, I noticed that there were an awful lot of faxes going back and forth between Tony and Kamm, but it wasn't until many years later I came to understand exactly what happened. Kamm was desperate to own the property and had gone behind our backs to ask the real estate agent to swap our names on the title for his. The real estate agent had known of Kamm's activities for years and refused to comply, so Kamm then asked the agent for our solicitor's name so he could call them and get them to change it. Again, the real estate agent refused. When he realized that he wasn't getting anywhere by going behind our backs, Kamm's next move was to contact Tony directly. He sent a series of faxes to Tony promising to write up a legal contract stating that the money we'd put into the property would be paid back to us whenever we asked for it or if we ever left the Order. He assured us that we were free to leave at any time. Since this was also stated in the Rule and Constitution, anything and everything that one put into the Order would be returned when one left, Tony considered the offer of the contract to be a fair deal. He immediately authorized the name change with the solicitor and swapped our names with Kamm's on the property title. Since Tony was always the one to look after all finances and legal matters, I had nothing to do with it, except when it came to sign on the dotted line when told to do so.

Kamm quickly organised the contract and shortly after Tony and I were called to the office to sign the document. Kamm had already signed the contract and had Malcolm Broussard witness it. Malcolm didn't allow us to read the contract before signing, though, so we signed on the dotted line before it was whisked away to the filing cabinet without us ever receiving a copy.

The settlement date for the house couldn't arrive quickly enough for Tony. He was chomping at the bit to prepare the property for the impending Chastisement. Early in 1997, Kamm had received urgent messages from the Virgin Mary warning that the Hale Bopp comet was going to hit earth during the first week of June, so all members were urged to prepare their houses by storing food and water. Tony wanted to move into the house as soon as possible, so he could prepare. No sooner were we in, then he tore out the shower cubicle. Although there were three large tanks connected to our house, Tony believed in saving as much water as possible so from then on all six of us had to share bath water. He wouldn't allow us to drain the water out afterwards either. He used a small jug to transfer the bath water from the bath to a 30-litre drum that sat beside the toilet. He disconnected the flush on the toilet and we used the bath water to flush the toilet. In addition to his obsession with saving water, Tony also had an intense dislike of mirrors, so when I decided the girls would have the bedroom that had a beautifully decorated mirror hung on the wall, he ripped it off the wall, saying it would only make the girls vain. "There's no need to be looking at yourself ever. It causes pride." The only mirror we had from then on was the tiny 20cm mirror in the bathroom, which the girls couldn't even see themselves in as they weren't tall enough.

We were warned that when the Hale Bopp comet collided with the earth it would burn everything, and people would be unable to venture outside due to the intense heat, fire and devastation. Once that passed we were warned that there would be extreme cold. The overriding message was that we, the "chosen people," would be safe if we followed the instructions of our superiors and it reminded me of my childhood and "The Warning." Only now I was an adult and the parent of four small children, which made the prediction feel both ominous and utterly impossible. Yet, no matter how skeptical I was, I couldn't discount it.

Our group of "chosen people" was to follow Kamm, as he was the head of all seers around the globe as well as the ultimate superior in our community. We were instructed to store as much tinned and dried food as finances would allow as well as bottled water since town water would be contaminated. The tank water was blessed and sprinkled with holy water to ward off any possible poisoning. Tony took it upon himself to go out and buy tin plates, bowls and mugs for us to eat off, since he said they would last forever.

And be the ugliest crockery on the planet, I thought to myself.

Since the Hale Bopp warning was just one in the string of many doomsday warnings, cult members had already been acquiring things for years; clothes from charity stores, tools that had been cast off, and other necessities from a variety of places. Garden sheds were full of these items that, we were told, would be in short supply once the comet hit. Tony trawled all charity shops in Nowra for old Army blankets to protect us from the freezing cold and we were advised to cover up our windows with black plastic or, even better, plywood to protect ourselves from heat from the Comet, and the demons that were to be released from Hell that would kill us if we looked at them.

As we began moving into our new house and preparing for the comet, I found myself feeling more and more fearful for myself and my children. My fears intensified when it was revealed that children would be "taken" to heaven for their safety during these Tribulations. When I asked for more detail regarding the children and babies being "taken," I was told that the children would just disappear without any trace. Since children were considered innocents, they would be taken to Heaven body and soul, and returned once the world was cleansed. This was also to prove to unbelievers in the world that there really is a God and that Kamm was truly His prophet. In addition to the preparations we were making, the community members that lived in permanent houses had to make room for other members who lived in the mobile homes, as the latter wouldn't be protected when the punishments arrived. So now, not only was I faced with impending doom, I also had to prepare myself to share my already crowded house with people I barely knew. There was nowhere to escape. Kamm and Jan made up the lists of who would be sharing quarters with whom, and when the list was renewed each year before every supposed catastrophic event, the names changed. It took me a long time to connect the fact that the rooming assignments depended on who was currently hanging out with whom and who was in or out of favor with Kamm.

The Major Queens were always assigned to stay with Kamm since he was their "mystical husband" and he claimed they would be safer with him. As the years wore on, I realized that we got a new warning about the world ending about every six months, so I was always on high alert to save food, clothes, and water and attend as many prayers as possible since it was drummed into us that this was the only way to hold back God's mighty arm.

This constant fear of impending doom also made it impossible for community members to plan beyond the next predicted end. In retrospect, I could see that this was exactly how Kamm kept us attached to the community. He would predict an end time, we would spend every waking hour preparing for it, and then when it didn't come, he would use it as proof that we were, in fact, the chosen people; the ones who escaped destruction and retribution again and again. This made us feel fortunate -- until the next warning arrived and we were thrown back into the cycle of preparing to live in a destroyed world.

Hale Bopp hitting the earth was predicted to be a big event and Kamm used this as an opportunity to make the main site at Cambewarra much larger by issuing special invitations from the Virgin Mary to people he wanted to live at Cambewarra. In 1997, during the last two weeks of May, there were a number of new arrivals from around the world, and I was curious to see what kind of people would come to live there.

Within a matter of days, we had four Canadians and what felt like an entire village of Maoris, who all appeared to be related. It took me a long time to understand that "family" for Maoris doesn't necessarily mean they are blood related. Instead, anyone who comes live with them for any length of time is considered family.

As the months passed, the community grounds became more crowded and more Maoris arrived. The Maoris were living in the former stables that had been done up as a series of separate rooms and were not suitable for a family at all. The stables were next door to Vito and having the Maori's living literally in his pocket did not make him happy at all. The Maoris had a very liberal view of life, belongings and routine, which caused many a heated row between community members. We soon learned that leaving anything lying around would essentially guarantee its disappearance.

Another constant bone of contention was the state of the amenities block. As there wasn't enough room in the stables for all of the Maoris, some of the older ones were housed in the mobile homes or caravans. Not having a bathroom or laundry of their own they shared the amenities block, which also included a laundry room, and since no one was assigned to clean it, the amenities was often left in a right mess. There were piles of dirty washing on the floor and clothes lines were often groaning with the weight of the washing that was hung on them. This didn't seem to bother the Maoris, but it definitely upset the other half of the community when half of the property was fairly well kept whilst the other half looked like bomb had hit it. The continued fights between members and constant complaints forced Kamm to remedy the situation by buying a house for the Maoris, so that they and their mess could be contained away from the rest of us. June 3, 1997 came and went with no doom in sight. The prediction was revised, and we were told that it could happen any time that week, and were warned to increase our prayers and sacrifices. When nothing had happened by the end of the month everyone relaxed --for a little while.

Meanwhile, despite the fact that we had moved a small distance away from the main property, the teenagers came over at all hours. They would invite themselves in and just begin talking. It felt like an interrogation rather than a conversation, and I resented the fact that they were trying to get as much information about me and my family as possible. According to them, everything that happened in my life previous to moving to the cult was preparation for being part of The Royal House.

Everyone constantly asking me if I was a Princess or not made me uneasy and anxious and all of the talk about queens, princesses and the Royal House did not make any sense to me at all until much later.

Once the hype of Hale Bopp died down Tony concentrated his efforts on "improving" the house to make it more self-sufficient. The house had a gas stove installed, but he deemed it a bad choice since gas would run out in the End Days. So, he set about searching for a wood-burning stove and eventually found one. Tony installed it and when we ate at home, rather than with the community, I had to cook on it. The stove was a money saving item for Tony since he got the wood for free, but it made cooking a time-consuming task for me and I resented the increase in my already overwhelming work load.

I was trying to keep my head above water as I looked after my kids, did my housework duties and fulfilled my community obligations. I was very reluctant to get too involved because not only didn't I like the place at all, but also because it took up all my time. I also disliked the fact that everyone knew what everyone else was doing all the time, and that we even had to ask permission to go to town to do grocery shopping. I disliked this latter directive so much that I resisted asking for as long as possible, but Tony didn't like it when I pushed the boundaries because it was a sign that I wasn't doing the right thing and he hated the idea that he'd be judged for my bad behavior.

Once Tony had completed his "property improvements," he threw himself in the community with gusto. All the men were rostered onto various shifts to work in Kamm's two shops; one in North Nowra, and the other at Ulladulla (an hour's drive away). It was Kamm's idea to buy these shops and have community members work in them for a basic wage because it generated a regular income that was used to fund community projects. As the community was working towards self-sufficiency, the money from the shops provided Kamm with the money he needed to buy hot houses, build a chapel to house the Gethsemane rock, build another chapel down on the Holy Grounds near the Shoalhaven River, and build a proper school building amongst other things that Our Lady had written about. According to Kamm, the property was going to be a mini-city. The younger people (and there were plenty of them at this stage, mainly Maoris) worked in the Ulladulla store, but Kamm didn't own this store for long as the kids didn't take the job seriously and customers complained about various things and Kamm ended up selling it at a loss. The North Nowra store was a small convenience store that had a large clientele from the primary school across the road before Kamm bought it, but Kamm's arrogance and the knowledge that he was a cult leader caused the store to lose business when he bought it, and while he managed to bring back some of the clientele, it was never the same.

I got to know an older gentleman, who worked in the North Nowra shop, quite well. He and his wife lived on the main property with one of their four children and the family was friendly and welcoming. The wife played the organ on Sundays and also taught some of the younger children in the improvised day care that Kamm set up. I noticed that even though they were both friendly to everyone, they didn't get too involved. In an effort to get to know each family better, Tony was eager to invite each family over for afternoon tea on Sundays so we could get to know everyone. He began by asking Maria. She smiled at us, shook her head and said, "Thank you so much for the invitation. You're a lovely family but we can't. It's not good for you to be seen with us." When I heard this, I was wondered what on earth she meant. Tony pressed for details but she refused to enter into any more conversation. She was always friendly but never visited.

The first school building was a small brick building a stone's throw from the chapel that was originally the caravan park's community room. Before the influx of members in June 1997, there were only a few children being taught there. Kamm's main reasoning for having a school there was that by having Government funding it would prove the property wasn't a cult and would make it easier for Bettina to get the kids to school.

According to Kamm, since Bettina was young, she was a bit flighty and unorganised thus he needed to help her with the kids. He claimed that he was always tired due suffering the pain of the crown of thorns during the night and getting little or no sleep. He wanted to make the morning routine easier by having the school only a few metres away, but he didn't have the money to pay proper teacher wages, so he used the services of Victor Soufflot, a retired school teacher who was part of the community but lived outside of the compound in Nowra township.

Victor and his sister, Mary, had never married and both were retired.

Mary volunteered her services in the office with Jan whilst Victor taught school. He suffered severe emphysema due to smoking in his younger year and his ill health made teaching a struggle. Initially, Victor oversaw the curriculum for a very small number of children whilst a few other members took turns helping him as teacher aides. It was an ongoing struggle for Victor to follow the school curriculum as he was pushed from all sides to create more and more time for religious education.

Kamm had even directed that in order for the children to become more familiar with living in a community, they needed to attend midday Mass and prayers then eat lunch with the rest of us before their afternoon lessons. The children's education was fast becoming a joke and I worried about whether my children would receive a useful education.

Meanwhile, seemingly unconcerned about the quality of our children's education, Tony meticulously gathered and read through the piles of messages that were printed out and placed on the back table of the chapel on almost a daily basis. We were informed of new prayers or practices that had to be implemented, either for penance for past sins or to gain a higher place in heaven or to outlast everyone else during the Chastisements. One of the more ridiculous edicts revolved around the Blessed Grapes. For someone who was always a cheapskate, it was amazing how quickly Tony pulled out his wallet to buy large jars with a screw top lid, kilos of grapes and bottles of brandy.

According to the messages, the Virgin Mary had instructed followers to fill as many large glass jars as possible with grapes and cover them with brandy, so that when the food ran out, one blessed grape a day would keep you alive.

Although I was taken aback by the requirement involving brandy, the process sounded easy enough. Put the grapes in the jars and cover them in brandy, what could be easier? As with everything involving religion, there was far more to the process. After buying the grapes, Tony washed them in plain water mixed with holy water (the holy water was supposed to kill any poisons the grapes had been sprayed with). After that each grape had to be cut from the bunch leaving a ¼" stem on each individual grape. Then holding a grape in one hand, each individual grape had to have the sign of the cross traced on it with a blessed grape that had been supposedly blessed by the Virgin Mary whilst saying the words, "In the name of the Father, and of the Son and of the Holy Ghost." Tony literally sat for hours doing this, until over a few sittings he had about a dozen litre jars full of grapes preserved in the back of the cupboard. I thought the whole thing was ridiculous, but since it kept him out of my way, I didn't protest -- much.

The day to day scheduling was very tiring since I rose early, began the day with prayer, fed the children, got them off to school, then hurried through my own household chores before attending to my community commitments. We'd been told that there would be a "break" at Christmas, so I was looking forward to a bit of a rest even if we weren't going actually going away for a holiday. Unfortunately, the break didn't include a rest from the prayer schedule, even if you went out for the day, you were still expected to complete all the prayers or show up for at least one chapel session.

Many community members were used to taking actual holidays each Christmas, so it came as a rude shock that holidays were a thing of the past. Kamm took to the pulpit admonishing us for even *thinking* we deserved a holiday when he was suffering 24 hours a day for us. He admonished us by saying that God's work was never done, and He never took a holiday. In order to quell the tide of complaints from "God's People," Kamm reluctantly allowed us to go out for day trips, but even that wasn't without a warning. Kamm would tell us we were free to go out and enjoy ourselves, *but* if a chastisement or punishment hit whilst we were out, then we wouldn't be saved. That was the deal, if you wanted to live in the New Holy Era, then you needed to be inside those gates adhering to all rules and prayers.

It was an unsettling way to live, but I was worried that if I didn't follow the rules to the best of my ability the effect on my children would be devastating and that they would blame me if they had to spend all eternity in Hell.

#

In April 1999 I gave birth to my daughter, Beth, on my own

birthday. It was a wonderful birthday gift since I felt more prepared and relaxed this time. There was a three-year gap between my last baby and this one, but within a couple of weeks Tony was grabbing my post birth belly, telling me that I was fat and to do my exercises to get back in shape. All the good feelings slipped away as I felt so inadequate and the tiny bit of self-esteem I had generated disappeared. There was no time to wallow in any of these feelings since community life demanded my attention.

When Beth was six months old, I fell pregnant with my next child. I hadn't expected to be pregnant again so soon and felt anxious about the future. It was the latter half of 1999 and the Y2K hype was building, but I didn't understand it. Kamm used this to manipulate the community with a multitude of "messages" spewing forth almost every day from a variety of "seers" who said the world the world would definitely end on New Year's Eve 1999. The Y2K bug was a sign that this era was over, and that we would awaken on January 1, 2000 to an entirely new world. Most of the community welcomed this news with open arms, it was what they had been waiting and preparing for years. The Queens were especially happy, since this meant that soon they would be living in the castles their Mystical Husband had promised them. At last Kamm would be seen as the true prophet he was. Finally, the chosen ones would be living life in the New Holy Era, while the earth and everyday life as we knew it would be completely different.

Of course, amongst these revelations, it was tarnished with reality. The reality that many tribulations would be coming to purify us in the meantime, not everyone would survive these chastisements, children and babies would just disappear without trace, but were told not to be sad. Our loved ones would be taken to heaven and be returned to us once the earth was cleansed and safe. As the mother of several young children, I was terrified that my children might possibly disappear with no visible trace.

While all of this made me incredibly anxious, I tried not to dwell on it too much because the possibility that this could actually happen was too scary.

By December 1999, we were engaged in continuous prayer, sacrifice, reading of heavenly messages and the practical preparations of storing food and water for what was to come.

Everyone was warned well ahead that we were all expected to be praying through the night, and while New Year's Eve celebrations had always been shunned, this year Kamm came down particularly hard. He said it was vital that all members stay within the confines of the property because God would show no mercy to anyone who disobeyed the prophet's orders. The threat of severe punishment was to show the world there truly was a God and he was very displeased with where humanity was headed and catapult Kamm onto the world stage as being God's Prophet and new leader. Every day we were reminded that the world was supposed to definitely end on January

1, 2000, and it made me more anxious by the day.

On the first day of 2000, the community breathed a collective sigh of relief as the warning, just like every other dire warning, proved to be a false alarm, and we headed back to our homes and familiar morning tasks. I breathed a sigh of relief, but knew that another warning probably wasn't far off.

My fifth daughter, Sue, was born in July 2000. She was the easiest birth of them all and as usual I was home the next day, and life returned to normal. As normal as it could be with seven children all under the age of ten, but we managed to establish a new routine and things ran smoothly. Eight days after Sue was born, my youngest brother, Augustine, was killed in a car accident in the early hours of the morning. I'd left home when Gus was only nine-years-old and we'd had very little contact since then. The cult didn't encourage family connections with non-believers, so I didn't go to his funeral because Tony didn't want me to and he told me we couldn't afford the trip. My biggest worry was that I didn't trust Tony to adequately look after the children.

Of course, once the community found out about Gus's death, messages from Heaven abounded from almost every seer on the property. These messages were supposedly from my brother who was now in heaven and sending messages to comfort me. Everyone felt the need to tell me these messages on a regular basis and I felt like I never had time or space to grieve in peace. Meanwhile, my quiet baby suddenly began crying all the time and for no reason that I could figure out. For the next ten months I lived on five hours of broken sleep a night due to her constant cries. During this most difficult time my weight plummeted as I struggled to keep up the day to day routine. I begged Tony for help several times, but he simply told me that I wasn't organised enough and that I needed to pull my act together, telling me that if I were properly organised, then I wouldn't need any help. He reminded me that it was the woman's job to look after the house and children and even had the audacity to keep pressuring me to get pregnant again.

During this time, Tony's gambling addiction became much worse. He had been gambling for years, but now he seemed to go to great lengths to avoid spending time with the family, if he wasn't at prayers, working or hanging out with other members, then he hid out in a corner of the house on the computer. It was during this time I began to go numb and it was years later that I realised this was when I first began to lose feeling and just exist. I lived on auto pilot, looking after all my kids and putting every else's needs and wants first. I worried constantly about my baby and did everything in my power to discover why my little girl was always crying. To top everything off, she broke out in eczema all over her body when she was nine-months-old and this just made her crying worse. I knew Tony could hear her cry several times a night, but he never got up to tend to any of the children in the night, telling me that he needed his sleep because he was breadwinner.

One cold, rainy September day as I came out of a shop a fellow cult member approached me, asking if I'd heard the news and that it seemed like World War 3 had started. I had no idea what he was on about but it certainly made me anxious.

When Tony picked me shortly after he informed me that there'd been a terrorist attack in the US. Being very ignorant of world issues and not understanding what a terrorist attack really was, I wasn't sure what to expect, nor how soon. When we arrived home, Tony put the television on and proceeded to spend the next few hours watching the horror unfold. The first few horrific pictures are still etched in my memory, it sickened me that human beings could be so cruel to their fellow mankind. I just couldn't watch it.

Nothing like a major world event to get the heavenly messages spewing forth again. Kamm and his worldwide seers were in overdrive, receiving messages left, right and centre that this attack was the beginning of the Final World War III. The World War to end all World Wars. New revelations from the Fatima messages, special insights never heard before. Once again we were on high alert to be ready for imminent punishments that would result from this terrorist attack. I could feel my anxiety rise another level and worried about my kids. Was now the time that some or all of them be taken? It hurt to think about it so I pushed the thought from my mind.

Meanwhile I'd made up my mind that I didn't want any more kids. Besides being completely overtired, I could see that Tony didn't care about me or the kids. I knew that. I wanted out, out of the marriage (although this was a subconscious thought) and out of the cult. I didn't have any direction or ideas of how to create the life I wanted, I just knew I wanted life to be better and different. The constant drudgery of everyday life, the pressure of the world apparently ending all the time, more prayers and sacrifices to be made, lack of enough money to buy all the necessary groceries, the weekly panic attacks at the supermarket checkout; it was all too much. Occasionally other community members invited me out for a coffee or to see a movie but every time I made excuses that the children needed looking after. The stark reality being that I didn't even have a coin to my name and was too embarrassed to say so. I literally kept going for the sake of my kids. I kept telling myself that one day, life would be very different.

I actually felt a sense of peace with my little decision, of course Tony knew nothing about it. It felt like I had just a *little* bit of control over my life. Then after just a few months when I thought I was home free, Tony began pressuring me for another baby. I wanted none of it. Out of the blue with no prompting from me he promised he'd change and would help me; "I suddenly realise that with this many children you need my assistance. So, I'll help you."

I fell for it and a few months later found myself pregnant again. A few months before I fell pregnant, I had been quite sick with bronchitis and still had a terrible, deep chested hacking cough that I couldn't shake. I tried everything natural, it didn't work. One of the "nuns" who was a seer, told me that Our Lady had mentioned Rosehip tea would heal me. I began drinking it but felt my lungs filling up and got really scared so stopped. I should have visited the doctor as it was obvious I had fluid on the lungs but Tony was against visiting doctors. During these months Tony showed no empathy at all, in fact he got angry every time I coughed, telling me that I was only making so much noise in order to attract attention. He even told me not to cough in the chapel where everyone could hear me. I was 5 months pregnant when my doctor overheard me coughing one day whilst I was waiting for my appointment and ordered x-rays. I must have been at the tail end of the infection, because the x-ray showed my lungs were clear and the cough ended soon after.

No sooner had my bronchitis healed than panic attacks began, although I didn't know they were called that. Several times over the following months I would be suddenly overwhelmed with severe anxiety, palpitations, my chest got tight and every time I closed my eyes to sleep, I felt like I was choking to death. Most often these began at night so there were some very long nights and even longer days. I developed a huge fear of giving birth, I honestly felt like I simply could not push out any more babies.

Another incident that caused my anxiety to skyrocket was when Tony lost Sue when she was only 19-months-old. One shopping day he had taken her and the two oldest boys to the hardware store whilst I did some other shopping with the girls.

We had agreed to meet back at our meeting place in a local book store after we'd finished our errands, but when Tony arrived he didn't have Sue with him. I asked him where she was and he just looked blankly at me and said, "I don't know, the boys were looking after her." My heart stopped, panic rose in my chest and I suddenly found it difficult to breathe. "What do you mean you don't know where she is? You had her with you when you left," I said trying to remain calm. He said he couldn't even remember taking her with him. Now I was not only scared out of my wits, but so, so angry with him. To add insult to injury, his first response to this emergency was not to call the police, but to call James Duffy, the "Angel Man," to get him to ask the Angels where she was. Many members used this as their first line of defense when they had lost something or someone, but this made me even more angry.

Tony told me to stay at the book store whilst he called James, but the shopkeeper, sensing something was wrong, offered to call the police. Tony came back and told me that James would call him when he had an answer, but I wasn't waiting about for him to phone. Sue was small for her age and very, very shy. All I could think about was how scared she must be and who might have taken her. I *had* to find her as soon as possible. I asked the shopkeeper to mind the other children whilst I went looking for her myself. It said a lot that, even in the midst of panic over a lost child, I trusted a complete stranger more than I trusted my children's father.

I'd asked Josh and Jakob what shops Tony had visited and I followed that route, frantically looking in all the shops as I went past. I must have looked like a mad woman with all the rushing around. My last stop was the hardware shop. I'd been busy praying like the clappers that my little toddler would be here, safe and sound. I ran through the store, searching each aisle. Suddenly I saw one of the older shopkeepers sitting on the floor with a child in her arms. The dress looked like Sue's. Relief washed over me and I wanted to cry, but I checked my tears and held out my arms to my little girl and hugged her tightly. My racing heart calmed as Sue snuggled into me. The shopkeeper told me that when she went past the aisle, she'd seen Sue standing there all alone. She'd asked Sue her name but Sue had remained silent. So, she picked her up and Sue had fallen asleep straight away.

Tony had already shown himself to be irresponsible when minding the children and now any shred of trust I'd had for him had evaporated. When I arrived back at the bookshop, the police met me, but left when they saw that I'd found Sue. When Tony called to let James know that Sue had been found, his response was that the Angels had told him it was a close call, but it was not yet her time to be taken. The incident really frightened me and from then on, I kept a close watch on all my children.

As members of the community, it was our responsibility to prepare for Atonement Day, which arrived on the thirteenth of every month. On Atonement Day, believers would come from far and wide to attend hours of prayers in preparation for an afternoon visit from the Virgin Mary. While I wasn't a fan of these events, I soon discovered that volunteering to prepare the food was much more interesting than spending hours in the chapel praying, so I soon made it a point to be on kitchen duty when Atonement Day rolled around. However, it wasn't easy juggling my motherly duties and helping out, so I would usually have at least one toddler hanging off of me and a baby in the pram.

Women were tasked with cooking a big lunch spread for the pilgrims, whilst the men were rounded up and prepped for security matters by James Duffy. James was an older man who had spent a short time in the Army and, because of it, had been chosen by the Virgin Mary to head up the community security force. One could tell that he was very protective of his position and disliked anyone else making suggestions, even if they might have better results. According to James, The Angels spoke to him directly about any security threats, and we could always tell when they were speaking as he would bow his head, perform the sign of the cross and go silent. Once he'd received the message, he would then proceed to repeat what the angels had supposedly told him. And if the angels weren't guiding him, he would fall back on messages from his dead son, Grant Duffy. On Atonement Day, James would station men with two-way radios at the gates and various other points around the property to keep an eye on any potential threats to Kamm.

The day would begin with prayers in the chapel then move downstairs where everyone would congregate for lunch and where Kamm would move through the crowd like a celebrity like before giving a public address during which the pilgrims hung on his every word. Once this was finished everyone returned to the chapel to pray in order to bring about a "vision and message" from the Virgin Mary. Kamm would be escorted up the front by Malcolm, James and various other important people. The community would begin saying the Rosary while Kamm went into a trance-like state and began repeating what the Virgin Mary told him. All those who had prepared lunch would be in a big hurry to clean up in order to make it to the chapel in time to hear the message. Jan's husband, Dick, who had once worked in radio, used his expertise to record the messages on two tapes (the reason he used two tapes was to ensure that if the Devil interfered with one transmission, the message wouldn't be lost). The instant the message was finished, Jan would dash to the back of the chapel to personally collect the tape from Dick, then she would spend hours in the office typing it up and getting Kamm to sign off on it, so it could be distributed to the rest of the communities; usually that night or, at the latest, the next day.

Soon after we arrived, one of the first Atonement Day messages mentioned my Christian name towards the end. I wasn't present to hear what was said, but had several visitors come to me immediately afterwards in a huge state of excitement, telling me that I had been chosen to be a Princess and wanting to know my special name. I was urged to visit Kamm straight away and ask if, indeed, it really was me that was mentioned and find out what was my "mission" was. Inwardly I was shocked, scared and anxious about what this all meant, while outwardly I laughed it off. If I was going to be forced to live here, then I wanted to stay on the peripheral. I saw this Atonement Day message as a way of forcing me to become more involved and I resented it. However, Tony had been in the chapel and upon hearing my name mentioned immediately followed Kamm out to ask him if it was indeed me, and when the answer was "yes," Tony told me that I was to write a letter to the Virgin Mary asking for my special name and my mission. I had no intention of doing any such thing and when pressed by others for the details I flippantly answered, "Xena, Warrior Princess." I naively thought that if I pretended it was a joke, then it would be enough to throw everyone off the scent and keep me far away from Kamm and his ridiculous messages. Unfortunately for me, the community members were tenacious and when curiosity got the better of a couple of them, they decided to ask the Virgin Mary themselves.

A few days after the Atonement Day message, my role was explained to me via a letter from Our Lady. It said that nothing was to happen now, but that in the New Holy Era I would help spawn a new race through Kamm. This was all to happen via his "Holy Embrace;" a special mystery that no one could understand right now. This revelation only served to confuse me and I spent the next week hiding out while crying to myself. This revelation made me even more determined to keep to myself as much as possible and spent a lot of time wishing I could turn back the clock and return to life in Melbourne where I had real friends and a modicum of freedom.

Shortly after my Atonement Day experience, Tony and I were handed a letter from Kamm. In it, Kamm stated that he had become aware of a problem that he needed to discuss privately and asked if he could come visit us. Knowing that Tony would ignore any objections I might have had, I said nothing. Once seated in our home Kamm proceeded to tell us that community members had reported that we were asking questions about The Royal House, and that this was not something that would be tolerated. He explained that unless all questions were directed to him, there would be misunderstandings that would result in a disturbance in the community and undermine the holy work being done. He told us that, in the past, members had left due to these types of misunderstandings, and he wanted to avoid that. Tony and I had already learnt through others that some former members had left abruptly (some quite recently) due to the issues surrounding the Royal House and when we asked about it, no one could or would give straight answers. I felt very uncomfortable talking about the Royal House because it felt really secretive and wrong -- much like being around Kamm did.

It was only years later, after I'd gotten hold of a document that specifically named myself and others in hierarchical order of importance that I realised Kamm was testing the waters that day to see if I would sleep with him.

Over time, there was an increase in messages and letters from Kamm urging people to pray and get themselves spiritually prepared to join the Order and take their Final Vows. Many Sundays he would take over the homily time during Mass to an hour-long sermon that focused on moving forward and taking the vows. He would often get quite frustrated at people's reluctance to fully commit to joining the Order because, according to him, the Catholic Church could not and would not sanction this new religious order unless people actually committed and took vows. He needed numbers to prove to the Vatican that this new way of life was working.

It was during 1998 that Kamm began pushing all those living on the property who hadn't yet joined the Order to do so. It didn't matter how long they'd lived there, Kamm made it clear that he was going to speed up the process, lump everyone in together and make them take their vows on January 1, 1999 and he tried to convince everyone that going ahead as one group of unified people would be best for the community as a whole. He backed up his decision by telling us that the Virgin Mary was sending him messages about how it had to be done.

All of this made me feel physically sick. Initially we'd been told that there was a 6 – 12-month novitiate period before we'd have to take actual vows, but since the date for our novitiate was never really set, I'd ignored it and hoped that they'd forget or, at the very least, it would be rescheduled. When we joined, we'd been given paperwork to sign and the office had never asked for it back, so I'd been secretly hoping that we would move out before we were required to fulfill our end of the bargain. Now the net was closing more quickly than I'd expected and I still had no way out.

The final straw was when we were told that after taking vows, we would all have to wear the full dreaded brown habit. I dug my heels in and told Tony I wasn't ready, and that I needed more time because I didn't feel right about doing it. I told him that if he wanted to join, then he could go ahead and join without me. He wasn't happy about this because, as a married couple, we were expected to take our vows together and now I was holding up the works. Tony tried to be patient and understanding, for a short time, at least, and eventually he wrote a letter to Kamm outlining the reasons why I wasn't willing to join and asking what other choices were there. Kamm replied with a six-page letter. He was annoyed that Tony had written in the first place and even more so because Tony mentioned people who had left the community. Kamm also wrote "As for us pressuring you and your wife, like those of the Lefebvre (SSPX) group or others, this is also out of order. No one has ever been forced to do anything." This was a lie and I knew it. In the very first letter Kamm wrote to Tony (when we were still in Montmorency), he mentioned entering the order on three different occasions.

He went on to explain that the vows a married couple would take are not perpetual but have to be renewed each year. If we weren't willing to proceed he suggested four other options:

1) We could become Fourth Branch members and live off the property, 2) He would buy another property (a small farm) and we could move there and build another community, 3) We could rent a property in town, at his expense, until all monies from the contract had been returned to us or 4) We could move to another community. Kamm wrote that Our Holy Mother had instructed him to provide us with these options and that we had till mid- December to make up our minds.

I was pretty keen to take advantage of the third option so we could get the hell out of there, start fresh and leave all this cult stuff behind us. However, Tony wasn't in agreement with my choice of options and even less happy to have such a troublesome, determined wife on his hands. His method of resisting any change was to refuse to get a job, so we were unable to afford a mortgage or even a move, and, again, I was left feeling like my only option was to stay.

During the rest of the year, Kamm did his best to coerce his "flock" into making their vows in January the following year. In the Rule and Constitution that Kamm and Broussard wrote together, (basing it loosely on other religious orders' constitutions) they had concocted a rule where all members, upon taking their vows were to sign a contract handing everything over to the order. This included all money earned by whatever means, we were only allowed to be "caretakers" of anything we owned or any inherited possessions. To this end he was also planning to have all our money go into the one central bank account; he would then allocate an allowance to each family or single person, as he deemed necessary for their living expenses.

Mountains of paperwork was laid out on the back table of the chapel for us all to take and fill out all personal details of how much we earned and how we spent it. I was not a happy girl, this *really* encroached on our individual privacy and I wasn't backward in telling Tony this either. The kids and I were already going without, if this was to be enforced I knew we'd be poorer than ever. I also wondered how Tony was going to hide his gambling addiction, I questioned him on this but as usual there was no answer. This was most definitely not what I had ever wanted and I was quite clear I didn't want to be a part of it. Over the coming weeks, I discovered there were others who kicked up a shindy about it too. There were a couple of people who owned their own businesses and they were not keen to have their profits shared by the community. And fair enough too. Kamm was inundated with so many complaints about his proposal that he was forced to delay the vow taking for another year. Much to quite a few peoples' relief, including my own. That didn't stop him openly berating us all from the pulpit, for at least an hour that Sunday.

For me the days blended into weeks, months and eventually years. I was always very busy with my kids, housework, prayers, rosters to help down in the kitchen. Tony never helped with anything around the house so the day to day running of the household was left to me, even though he was around most of the time. Due to the community supposedly becoming self-sufficient, or at least working towards it; I was encouraged to utilise my country skills in baking bread, sewing clothes for myself and my children, making jam, chutney, jerky and taking a turn weeding the veggie garden in the hot house. All this squeezed in between my other everyday duties.

As a group there were times when we'd all eaten dinner together downstairs under the chapel. It was an on again, off again event due to various complaints from a select few. Kamm was determined though, to have us eating together as a community on a regular basis. He even told me one day in passing that he fully intended for us all to be having breakfast together as well. In the heyday of this community there were 180 people eating downstairs, it was one huge feat to prepare two meals a day for this crowd. In addition to this we had to menu plan and this was a nightmare. Not just in the amount of food to order and cook but there always seemed to be complaints about what was dished up. There was always somebody who didn't like something. Jan's husband, Dick, who had undergone at least one heart operation complained every single meal time about the amount of fat he found on his plate.

As time passed, I learnt to keep my eyes and ears peeled as I went about my business and not say too much. Over the years I'd pieced together information that I overheard, things that I saw and figured out that the Queens were single young girls, preferably pretty virgins who were chosen to spawn a new race, "mystically" with Kamm. This was supposed to happen only in The New Holy Era but there were "mystical" babies arriving already to Queens and also some Minor Queens (married) who were reportedly chosen by The Virgin Mary. Princesses were married women also, whose husbands allowed them to have babies with Kamm, in the New Holy Era and later on the title of Baroness was added. Between 1997 and 2000 there were many details that I heard but didn't quite understand then all of a sudden it came together.

It was January 2000 when I discovered what was really going on. Kamm couldn't wait for the New Holy Era and had decided that certain Queens who were "chosen by Our Lady" were now worthy to begin birthing "mystical" children. Kamm would secretly sleep with them without the knowledge of his second wife, Bettina. Almost every weekend he would take one or two away with him to Wollongong to stay at a hotel under the guise of Kamm visiting his four children from his first marriage. He usually took one older girl/woman and one younger in order for the older, more experienced one to show the younger girl how he liked to be pleased. As I watched various peoples' behaviour, over time all the pieces fell into place. I was horrified, disgusted, angry. In fact, I was *so* incensed that I wanted to physically hurt Kamm when I found out. I made it very clear to Tony that I'd had enough and didn't want to live there anymore, that it just wasn't right what Kamm was doing. Tony as usual ignored me and when I kept on about it, vainly tried to convince me that Kamm was a prophet and the rules were different for him because the Virgin Mary had told him so.

At this time, I wasn't aware of the law regarding the age of consent. For me it was morally wrong through and through and I didn't want any part of it. Around this time a document came into my hands that confirmed what I'd already worked out. That several of the young teenage girls had indeed been impregnated by Kamm but it was to be kept secret, especially from Bettina. In addition to this I discovered some married women had already birthed children fathered by Kamm and in one case, the woman's husband knew Kamm was sleeping with his wife, in their marital bed. When she gave birth to these children, the husband appeared happy to play along being the father to these children.

The more I found out, the angrier I became. What I really struggled with was the literal web of deceit surrounding Bettina. Kamm had almost everyone wound around his little finger, lying for him and soothing Bettina if she accidentally saw something that gave her cause for suspicion. How I longed to tell her the truth! So many times, I was tempted to walk over to her house and tell her everything and I told Tony so, too. The only thing stopping me was that I had no idea how to deal with the fallout and as much as I desperately wanted to move, had no friends to turn to nor funds to do so.

Discovering this awful truth caused me to keep to myself more than ever. Although I was friendly to everyone, I was very careful who I spoke to and what I talked about. I watched people like hawks and kept my distance from the ones I knew I definitely couldn't trust in any way, shape or form. I couldn't believe that that all these people thought it was ok to hurt Bettina on such a large scale.

Life became more of a struggle because I was mentally distancing myself more and more from the group. I was busy with all my kids, housework and attempting to keep up appearances in the cult. Attending prayers, eating as a group and helping out on the roster where it fitted in with my babies' schedules. By this time, we were eating the night meal downstairs and I hated every single minute of it. It was a big rush for me to bath all the children, feed the baby, tuck her into the pram, gather them all together and walk downstairs to eat. It was especially difficult during the winter months when it was cold and wet. Yes, we were still expected to attend dinner, even though it was difficult because we were fulfilling what the Virgin Mary was asking. Once home it was time to change the children into their pajamas and prepare them for bed. There was never any time to relax. Everything was made harder than normal due to the fact that we were supposed to get used to doing things by hand as well so it wouldn't be such a huge adjustment when there was no electricity in the End Days. Even such a simple task as using the washing machine...Tony wanted me to reuse the washing water so the water from the first load of washing would be caught in a large drum and I had to bucket it back into the washing machine for the next load. As the only person who did all the washing, I lifted these heavy buckets of water day in, day out. Even when pregnant or having just given birth. For sixteen years straight, I washed cloth nappies every single day and dried them without a dryer. If we had rainy or humid weather, all wet clothes and nappies would hang on racks in front of the wood fire, overcrowding our already small lounge room. Sometimes there was so much washing to get dry, that I would hoping there was a nappy dry in two hours so the baby would have a clean nappy to wear. Everyday life in general was made harder than it had to be so I was in a constant state of nervous anxiety in order to get everything done.

#

My sixth daughter, Ellie, was born in early August 2002. Her birth was awful, a very painful and drawn out affair, no doubt brought on by the extreme fear and panic attacks in the months preceding. It certainly made me more determined to never have any more kids. As usual I was home after 24 hours, but this time I was expecting the promised help from Tony.

Things were looking hopeful on the Sunday, he cooked dinner and organised some things for the next day. Monday morning arrived, the kids were off to school and I went to lie down, asking Tony to please do the washing.

"I'm off to do *real* work, not stay home to do the work you're supposed to do," he coldly replied as he disappeared out the door for the day.

Shock and anger welled up inside me, I was so stunned I couldn't even cry. How could have I fallen for his false promises, *again*? How could he be such a cold-hearted bastard and just walk away? I was so angry at myself for ever believing his false promise of change and now being back to square one yet again. As I dragged my aching body off to do the housework, I remembered all the times he had deserted me. I counted up the times he'd abandoned me physically and emotionally, and realized that the number was greater than that of the times he'd supported me. My life was a mess that I couldn't seem to find my way out of. My children relied on me to look after them. I sat down to breast feed my new baby when out of nowhere the after pains cut through my stomach like a hot knife and I thought I was going to pass out. My body shook so badly I had to put my baby down before I dropped her. Tony frowned upon painkillers, the more suffering you took on, the higher your place in Heaven after you died. I huddled beside my pink bundle, trying to sleep, but being unable to due to the extreme pain and hundreds of thoughts running through my mind.

Shortly afterwards, Tony called and when I asked him why, he replied in an off-handed manner, "Oh there are a couple of police cars on the driveway and they are interviewing people." I knew there had to be more to it than what he was telling me, and there was. It appeared that Kamm had been on the police radar for quite some time because of his activities with young girls and because of the rumour that guns were hidden on the property. Authorities had become concerned in late 1999, when it became obvious that there were massive holes being dug around the property.

Kamm explained that he had arranged the excavation of these holes for rubbish disposal in preparation for the coming chastisement when the rubbish trucks wouldn't be running. The police didn't believe him and said they were concerned about the safety of the community members because they'd been told there were guns hidden on the property. There were no guns on the property at that time, but it was ironic that the day the police visited the compound, Tony begun to work on securing a cupboard specifically to house a gun that Kamm was planning to buy.

That same day Kamm was arrested. He was handcuffed, and the police were asking questions about the women who'd had children with Kamm and they were now interviewing them, one by one. James Duffy was mad as a hornet because Sandra was one of the first to be interviewed and gave some details that were supposed to have been kept secret.

"Kamm will be incriminated," James told Tony and I, and I got the feeling that not even the Angels that James claimed to conjure could stem this tide. The cult was in a frenzy over the next few weeks as details emerged, and Kamm was charged. As Malcolm and Jan worked overtime to cover for their boss, they became more suspicious and secretive. The remaining Queens were ordered to keep their mouths shut and a very low profile. Kamm hired Greg Stanton, a lawyer who visited the community on a regular basis, held mock trials to assist those who would be taking the stand to get their stories straight, and encouraged community members to keep secrets and lie to the authorities in order to protect Our Lady's prophet.

Although his arrest had obviously shaken him, Kamm still came out fighting. He took to the pulpit almost every Sunday simultaneously berating and forgiving those who had "betrayed" him. He told us that Our Lady had predicted this "test," and that it was necessary in order to sort the wheat from the chaff; the real believers from the fake. We were encouraged to take pity on any members who left the community because they weren't strong enough to withstand the test. Only the true believers, God's faithful ones would remain. We needed to truly live according to God's laws and follow everything Our Lady asked of us and then the Victory would follow.

Lunches and dinners had been put on hold so mingling with community members was at a minimum. This didn't bother me, since I was busy with my newborn baby and my other children. I was very thankful I didn't live on the main property and was able to remain quite out of it. Quite frankly, I hoped Kamm *would* be going to jail, preferably forever, because he deserved it. My other hope was that the whole group would be disbanded, thus allowing everyone to move and give me a chance to get out of the community.

It shocked me when Tony came home one day only a few weeks later to tell me that Sandra and Michael were moving. It had only been about a month since Kamm's arrest and Sandra was one of his strongest supporters. She was always in his office and looked for every opportunity to chat with him. Tony had been spending quite a bit of time over at their house lately, too much time for my liking. He seemed to hang on their word. Ever since we'd moved to the cult Tony had tried to convince me that the Mathison's were a lovely family and encouraged me to get to know Sandra better. Whilst

Sandra was outwardly always friendly, my gut told me not to trust her. Over time through various little things she'd mentioned in conversations, I'd figured out that some of her children had been fathered by Kamm.

Sandra cooperated with police to a certain point, but then she and Michael abruptly moved their family to Queensland and made no attempt to contact anyone. Although police wanted to question them further, they refused to participate in the investigation. Nearly all the Queens were questioned and although there was much that came out, a lot more remained hidden. Everyone that was intimately involved with Kamm, was running scared, lying and burning evidence.

After Kamm's arrest, messages from the Virgin Mary were everywhere coming from everyone with urgent advice for the community to stay calm. Kamm was innocent, this was a test of everyone's faith in Our Lady's Prophet. Kamm wouldn't be going to jail. He was being safely cocooned by Our Lady. We were told that anyone that had left or were to leave in the near future, were weak anyway and needed to be weeded from the pack. Despite Kamm's sermons on forgiveness, anyone that decided to move was shunned. The in-fighting grew worse, so I retreated and kept busy with my children.

Despite the looming court case and possible jail time he faced, Kamm wouldn't be deterred from gathering his flock and making one more attempt to force us all to take vows and consolidate finances. This time he decided to use the talents of a woman who had once worked as a parole officer in Canada.

Pamela was very loud, overbearing, tactless and disliked by the community. Since arriving, she'd worked to gain Kamm's trust so that she could be part of the Inner Circle, and although the term was no longer used publicly, it definitely still existed. Eventually Pamela convinced Kamm that the best way to ascertain if members were in the right frame of mind to take the vows and move the Order forward, was to create a panel that would interview everyone, and she nominated herself to be a part of the panel with Broussard and Kamm completing the trio.

When the memo was put out regarding these interviews, there was a lot of unrest between members. There were papers to fill out beforehand where they asked quite a bit of personal information. I knew that any extra information the office could get their hands on, would in some way be used against us at some point. I was vehemently against it this time and was more forthright in telling Tony this. He was angry that I seemed to always be trying the thwart our family's attempt to go forward in joining the Order and told me that I was the only one having trouble conforming. I didn't care, I did everything I could to avoid taking vows that tied me to this dreadful place.

Quite by accident I discovered that another woman was also bucking the system. Although we weren't close I admired this woman because she was often seen as a trouble maker, speaking up against things she considered trampled on our freedom. It felt really good knowing I wasn't the only one who was digging their heels in and I'd found out that Tony was liar. He wasn't happy when I went home and told him that I wasn't the only one against joining the Order.

The interview day dawned, and I was anxious because I could feel the noose tightening around my neck. I hated to be in the same room as Kamm, Broussard and Pamela, and since married couples were interviewed together, Tony came with me. He always took charge in the talking department because he didn't trust me to say the correct things. I was too fiery and too blunt, and, according to Tony, it put people off. Pamela and Kamm were their usual over friendly selves, Broussard crouched behind the desk clutching his crucifix in silence deferring to Kamm, as always.

Kamm opened the conversation with his usual smart- mouth humour designed to make us feel at ease. He then launched straight into describing his plan for everyone taking vows, bringing forward plans to join Eastern and Western Catholicism, (which had never been done, and for good reason) by ordaining married men as priests and bishops. As Tony had spent a couple of years in the SSPX seminary, he was top of the list of candidates. However, Kamm stressed publicly and privately, that those men wanting to be ordained had to have to permission from their wives. He already knew I wasn't keen about any of it, but Tony answered positively for both of us. Knowing that the wearing of the habit was a big stumbling block for me, Kamm tried to reassure me that it wasn't coming in straight away, but being well aware of his track record of forcing his constituents to obey, I wasn't convinced.

Pamela asked her own probing questions to which Tony replied without giving away too much. Thankfully the ordeal didn't last long, but once we had left, I felt a stone in my heart and anxiety in my stomach, it had never been my intention to join a religious order, let alone a weird group like this.

It took nearly a week or so for everyone to complete their interviews, and in the meantime the gossip flew around the community at a hundred miles an hour. Although Kamm had told Pamela to keep the information confidential, everyone knew the chances of that were low, and the truth that members hadn't said in the office to the "Three Musketeers" was now being verbalised behind their backs.

While all of this was going on, I received a phone call out of the blue from Scottie. My family had known Fr. Peter Scott since 1979, when he'd converted to Catholicism. Coming from Protestantism he'd felt it necessary to take the harshest road in order to be the best Catholic he could by fasting, praying, reading as much as possible. He had decided to become a priest so he could help spread the Catholic Faith and was ordained in 1988, as a priest of the Society of St. Pius X, (SSPX). I was happy to hear Scottie's voice. He had visited my family many times over the years, so we knew him very well. He'd been sent to Goulburn in New South Wales to resurrect their flailing Australian seminary, and since we hadn't seen each other for such a long time, he proposed coming to visit us in Nowra. My gut told me that he had intentions of trying to convince us to leave and I was hoping that he'd be able to talk some sense into Tony, since he refused to listen to me. I enthusiastically invited him for the next Sunday and eagerly looked forward to his visit.

Besides a few grey hairs Scottie hadn't changed much. My siblings and I had always enjoyed his sense of humour, it was great to laugh again. Tony frowned upon my sense of humour and laughter because he considered it flirting, but I had no idea what he was talking about. Scottie took great interest in the children's schooling and asked what was going on in the community. Tony was never one for detail and skirted around the issue, making out that although Kamm had been arrested the members remained tight and committed. Scottie outlined his grand plans for the Seminary, which included quite a lot of building and renovating. Knowing that Tony had building experience and was very good at it, Scottie offered him a job. I was so happy to hear this because if Tony took it up, it meant he would be spending less time in the community. Tony thanked him and told Scottie he would think about it. Scottie also invited us down to attend Mass sometime.

After Scottie left I encouraged Tony to seriously consider his offer of work. Tony was concerned about the three- hour travel time, but since Scottie had offered him the use of the workers cottage to stay over a few days, I suggested he take it. Eventually Tony decided that he could work at least three days, staying over two nights. This made me happy not only because I was hoping that the more time Tony spent around Scottie and other Traditionalists, he would come to see the ridiculousness of this community we were living in, but also because it meant I would have three blessed days without having to cater to a husband who didn't seem to care about me.

Once Tony was out I secretly rang Scottie to tell him the good news. He was very happy to have Tony on board and organised for him to start the next week. What was supposed to be a quick phone call, turned out to be much longer. I suddenly found myself opening up to Scottie and telling him everything that was going on, my marriage problems, what was going on in the community, wanting to move. I was relieved that someone was actually listening to me. There were no immediate solutions, but at least I'd offloaded some worries.

A few months beforehand, Tony had mentioned to me that although he wasn't considering the priesthood just yet, he wanted to go celibate. I was quick to agree, sex wasn't something I'd ever looked forward to, it was completely unfulfilling, it only ever happened when he wanted it and I'd already decided I didn't want any more children. Only recently when I'd asked Tony for help with the children, he responded, again, with "I'm only here to help you if you really need it. If you were more organised you wouldn't even be asking me for help. So organise yourself better." My heart froze over in that moment and I knew the kids and I were on our own whatever the future held.

In one of my phone conversations with Scottie, I'd confided that I didn't want any more children. He reproached me for thinking in such a manner, it wasn't Catholic and Catholic wives should keep having children until they couldn't have any more. Besides I wasn't allowed to refuse my husband if he wanted sex. I was taken aback and hurt because I'd confided so much to him and thought he understood my predicament and it was crushing to find that the religious edicts would always take precedence over my own needs.

I felt really confused about what to do. I was determined not to have any more children, yet I felt guilty for taking charge of my life and making this decision. It had been drummed into me from a very young age that men were the head of the house, you did as you were told while your desires and goals took a back seat. And if you asked a priest for advice, then you were bound to follow it, putting aside all your own feelings and thoughts. Despite the promise of a higher place in heaven, I still didn't want any more babies. I thought about it so much that my brain hurt trying to justify my decision, it was difficult to bend Catholicism to fit my desires, so I decided to just leave it and see what happened. I didn't tell Scottie or Tony about any of this, but I really did feel alone.

The one thing about not deciding is that, one way or another, a decision ends up getting made. I learned this the hard way. After months of no affection or emotion towards me, one morning before work Tony suddenly came onto me. I resisted and asked him why on earth he was doing this when he'd decided he wanted to be celibate. He wore me down by telling me that whilst he'd been celibate he'd been "inspired" to have another child. Everything that Scottie had told me about being a good Catholic wife flooded through my head and guilt set in, so I begrudgingly went through with the act. Afterwards I felt like I'd lost the little bit of confidence I'd built up in the preceding months, and soon enough I found myself pregnant again. I told myself, this one would *really* be the last.

When I announced to Tony that I was pregnant again, he was really happy. For a little while at least. He had taken me aside shortly before to tell me that he believed he was depressed.

After reading a newspaper article describing the symptoms, he was wondering what to do. I understood nothing about depression but instinctively knew it was beyond my scope of expertise so told him I would go to the doctor with him. Some years before in a rare moment of honesty he'd revealed to me that as a teenager he'd often thought of suicide. He'd mentioned then that everybody thought of suicide at some point in their lives. In my naivety I had absolutely no idea the severity of what he'd told me about suicide but something I *did* know for sure was that not everyone thinks of suicide. I certainly never had. I had enough to deal with at this point and thinking of my safety and the children's, mentally removed myself. I did attend the doctor's appointment with him because I knew damn well Tony wouldn't tell the entire truth. And I was right. It was up to me to describe and explain everything to the doctor, who promptly prescribed medication.

I was keeping to myself a lot these days and avoiding the community as much as I could without raising any suspicion. I could feel myself mentally detaching from the people and avoided attending prayers and sometimes mass too. Due to striking up the friendship with Scottie again I was wanting to travel to Goulburn for mass, Tony wasn't keen because he was scared Kamm, Pamela and Broussard would find out. Then they'd realise we had interests elsewhere, thus putting our Order beliefs on shaky ground. Despite Tony's misgivings, I made the trip down to Goulburn quite a few times with the kids. I may have had very few choices but I was going to do my own thing as much as possible.

The kids and I quite liked this new routine of Tony going off to Goulburn to work. He was gone for a few days at a time each week which took the pressure off us. I'd slack off on attending community prayers and spend more time at home. I could really feel the tension rise when he was in the house. In an effort to separate myself further from the cult, I'd decided that this baby I was carrying would not be baptised by Broussard and told Tony so. He felt uncomfortable about it but I didn't care.

Scottie would come to the house and do it as soon as I was home so that by the time the community found out, the deed would be done.

I began to feel the urge to purge the house of all the old fashioned, now unnecessary items we'd been saving for the End of the World. Each time Tony went away, I got rid of more stuff. One of the first things to go were our religious "habits", the ones we were supposed to wear when we took our final vows. They'd been hanging in our cupboard for long time now, making me feel sick and anxious every time I saw them. One day after Tony had left for Goulburn, I took the pile of hideous clothing out to the chicken pen, heaped them on the ground and set fire to them with the help of some petrol. Oh my god it felt *absolutely wonderful* to do that! I felt huge satisfaction watching the flames burn that clothing to a crisp. It had been a long time coming.

I was once again suffering from panic attacks as a result of reading "The Beautiful Side of Evil" by Johanna Michaelson. The title had piqued my interest when I looked over Tony's shoulder as he was ordering books online. As soon as it arrived, I sat down to read, it was both horrifying and fascinating. I couldn't put it down, but it scared me so much I could not sleep for a week. I spent every night attempting to sleep on the couch, but each time I closed my eyes I thought I would choke to death.

The book lifted the veil on a psychic surgeon running a cult group in

Mexico and while my experience and the authors were completely different, the one thing I was certain of when I finished reading that book was that I knew I was in a cult and somehow I had to get myself and my kids out of it.

Due to Kamm's arrest and ongoing criminal trial, Tony was wondering if our property was at risk of being sold from underneath us in order to pay for his court costs. I raised the question of the document we'd signed when Kamm had the title changed, we were never allowed to read it nor received a copy. I suggested asking for a copy but Tony wasn't going to ask for it because it he believed it would raise suspicion on their part that we weren't believers anymore and that we were at least thinking of leaving.

At this point I couldn't have cared less what they thought, every day I was mentally removing myself more and more. I still had no idea how I was going to leave, I was expecting a new baby in a few months, I had no money, even my welfare payments weren't mine. Tony had always filled out the papers and got me to sign them, then the funds went into his account. He half-heartedly began looking for similar properties around our area that "maybe" we could move to. He found one that was even further out into the bush than we now were and was more advanced in self-sufficiency. Thankfully we didn't have the money for a deposit because in my mind, when we moved we would be leaving the cult, the members and beliefs far, far behind. Besides, I'd had enough of living the country, I wanted to be in the suburbs.

Meanwhile Kamm was moving forward with ordaining married men as priests and bishops, even though it was against the Catholic Church's teachings. Broussard had been sent overseas to meet a rogue bishop who consecrated him in a secret ceremony. It all happened so fast he was back within the week. Kamm was eager for Broussard to use his new powers as soon as possible but publicly and privately assured all wives that any married men who were wanting to receive priestly orders *must* have the written permission of their wives. I relayed all this to Scottie who was horrified that Kamm was actually going through with it. I was thankful that Tony was spending quite a bit of time in Goulburn. I knew that he was wanting to one day be ordained but that was going too far, far in the future, if at all, if I had anything to do with it.

During the preceding months, Tony had become more and more withdrawn from the kids and I, but he appeared to have plenty of time and energy to spend hours with cult members when he wasn't at Goulburn, and the time he was at home he spent in front of the computer gambling. Almost every night he wouldn't come to bed until 3 or 4am. I confronted him about his gambling habit, but he just got angry and walked away. Once I even surprised myself by hearing the words, "If you keep this up you'll lose your family," come out of my mouth. To which he responded, "I don't take kindly to threats." I discovered through listening to others' conversations that Tony was spending quite a bit of time chatting with a couple of "seers" and also in the office which made me suspicious about his actions. I had a nagging feeling that something was afoot.

One morning in May my world was shattered. We were drinking coffee and as he gulped down his last drop, without looking at me, he casually mentioned that he'd decided to become a sub-deacon. And that the only reason he was telling me is because the office was putting up a list of the men who would be receiving subdiaconate orders in the next fortnight. I was so stunned I couldn't speak. I felt anger welling up inside me. Anger towards him, anger towards Kamm and Broussard. For months they had assured everyone from the pulpit that this was going to be above board, every wife had to give permission and here Tony was, doing exactly what he liked. I pushed all my emotions down as I quietly asked him about it. I had learnt early in our marriage that I wasn't going to get anything out of him if I showed any emotion at all. He had always hated any questioning or confrontation about his actions, so he answered me as briefly as possible before disappearing out the door to "work."

I tried to process the news as I went about my housework. So many thoughts running through my mind, so many emotions running through my body. I was infuriated and very, very hurt. How dare he. He knew he had to ask and he *knew* I'd say no. So, he went behind my back and arranged it anyway. Some weeks later I discovered that he'd asked questions of one of the seers he was close to, about becoming a sub-deacon then a priest and apparently all the messages had told him yes. I was very angry at her too for being all friendly and understanding to my face, but secretly supporting Tony and encouraging him, without considering my thoughts or feelings on the matter.

I wasn't looking forward to going down to the chapel for prayers later that day. I didn't want to see a single soul. When I entered the chapel there was The List, and it had Tony's name on it. I felt all the emotions engulf me again. I decided to wait for Broussard and when he arrived to prepare for mass, I asked to speak with him privately. I was usually quite friendly, so he could tell something was wrong. Clutching his crucifix, he sat down while I remained standing. I told him that Tony had only just informed me, that morning, of his decision to become a sub- deacon and that I was angry about it. I was angry because he didn't obtain my permission and I had been assured that it was protocol that I be asked. I never agreed to Tony becoming a priest and they knew that. Broussard had always been spineless, and he was no different now as he sat there, silent and expressionless. When I paused to breathe he told me that Tony could do whatever he wanted because the priesthood was his "vocation." As he got up to leave, I felt my anger welling up again, how *dare* he trample over my feelings! I don't even know where it came from, but suddenly words were coming out of my mouth. I heard myself saying to him, "You do realise that this will split up our marriage?"

Malcolm just shrugged his shoulders and said, "I don't care. It's not my problem." My anger boiled and I longed to hit him. He saw my anger and took off before I could say or do anything further and avoided me completely from then on.

The next two weeks were an emotional hell for me. I felt like I was being forced to accept something I knew was wrong. Tony cut me off emotionally and chose to spend even more time with the cult members, and I was angry at the world. I found it difficult to accept that my so-called husband didn't respect or love me enough to ask me my opinion. I was devastated on every level but kept myself together as much as I could for the sake of the children. When I was alone, the tears poured out. My foundation had been completely rocked, and I felt like the whole community was against me. I couldn't trust anyone. I still showed up for the necessary cult things, but ensured my appearances were brief so I could be a recluse at home. The few members that I did run into tried to make light of the situation and laughed off my feelings. They tried to convince me that my initial shock would pass and I'd get used to it. "If only you would let go of your will, everything will be ok. Leave it in God's hands." Hearing that just made me angrier. Not one person understood me or even tried to listen to what I had to say. I felt totally alone. Tony continued to be cold towards me, and the more questions I asked, the more he ignored me. His personality completely changed when he was in the community, he was quite happy talking to everyone else and preparing for the ceremony. And he fueled my rage by spending hundreds of dollars on the necessary special vestments and books in order to be prepared.

Word got back to Kamm that I had taken the news very badly and despite others' trying to convince me otherwise, I was still against Tony going forward with the ceremony. So, he wrote me a letter, telling me he would take Tony's name off the list and that Tony would only be ordained if I expressly permitted it. My initial feelings upon reading this letter was one of relief but then I knew there'd be some price to pay for this. After days of weighing up the options, I felt guilted into giving permission for Tony to go ahead.

The dreaded evening of May 22, 2004 arrived. I'd felt physically ill and anxious all day. My insides were torn in two, suddenly the phrase, "like a lamb led to slaughter" was crystal clear to me. God knows why, but at the time I thought I had to attend the subdiaconate ceremony in order to support my husband despite not agreeing with it. I was the only one sitting up the front and it bloody well nearly killed me. Everyone kept their distance. Tony was excited and looking forward to this step that he'd been refused in the seminary all those years ago. "For a bloody good reason," I thought to myself. Thank goodness the children weren't there to see how upset I was, it was an evening ceremony and I'd left my eldest in charge at home. Normally I had excellent self-control regarding tears or shock but this night I was literally torn apart. I absolutely could *not* hold myself together, no matter how hard I tried. I was silently hysterical all night, sobbing quietly as the ceremony went on around me. I also knew deep in my heart that the marriage was completely over, and while I didn't want to be married to Tony anymore, I did still want to follow the rules and beliefs I'd been raised with, but the pressure to maintain a marriage to a man who didn't care about me or his children was more than I could bear.

The ceremony seemed to take an eternity, I was emotionally spent when it finished and just want to escape everyone to go home. Tony was on a high that made me feel more ill than ever. Other members tried to give me consoling hugs but it actually made me feel worse. And they were still on banging on about "you'll soon get used to it." Although I attempted to smile through my tears my thoughts were far from friendly, lucky no one was able to read my mind. Tony and I walked home silently across the paddock in the dark and when we were in bed, I asked him what was the real reason for him becoming a sub-deacon when he knew I was completely against it. I knew he was grateful for the darkness because he thought it would be easier to bullshit me. In an effort to tell me what he thought I wanted to hear, he proceeded to spin the story that he had only wanted it a little bit and had been mostly "forced" into it because he needed to be "seen to be doing the right thing, to keep the unity." This was his latest catch phrase that annoyed me no end. He constantly talked about "the unity of the community" that apparently came before your wife or family. I was always a very honest, black and white girl who liked to talk things out. If I didn't understand something, then there was nothing I liked more than sitting down to listen to all sides in order to understand a subject better. But lie to me and it's all over. Lying there next to him, I *knew* he was fibbing to me. I inwardly berated myself for being weak and going against my gut, allowing myself to get hurt yet again.

Always a believer that a good sleep makes everything look better in the morning, I'd hoped that I would feel happier when I woke up. That it was all a bad dream. Reality slapped me in the face as soon as I opened my eyes. I really began to withdraw more and more from the community. I didn't know what do, who to ask for advice, I had no money at my disposal and my baby was due in a couple of months. I decided to lay low for now and take one thing at a time.

One decision that I made then and there was that I would explore the option of going to Sunday mass in one of the churches in the local parish. Kamm had told us many, many times from the pulpit that if we ever attended mass in any outside churches, we'd be shunned. The priest wouldn't give us holy communion and we'd be publicly shamed. I thought I'd take the kids and go find out for myself, it'd have to be better than facing the community every day. Tony didn't like my idea, he said he couldn't be seen coming with me in case it got back to the community. So, the very next Sunday, the kids and I went to mass together. It was difficult to walk into the church and see everyone watching me but we found ourselves a pew at the back and sat down. I didn't go to holy communion because I feared humiliation. However, some of the parishioners whispered "hello" and "welcome" to me as they went out the door after mass. Their kindness brought tears to my eyes. When we went outside, the priest extended his hand and introduced himself. I was a little shocked! He also told me I was welcome anytime.

I left thinking that clearly Kamm had it wrong. These people seemed kind and understanding.

A month or so after Tony's subdiaconate orders, Kamm organised one-on-one meetings with everyone in the community because he needed to know people's thoughts on the community after the initial ordination. He was also still banging on about "unifying and moving the community forward" for real this time. Now that the ordinations had begun, Kamm was looking at making each community self-sufficient in every way and wanted to start more communities because each property needed to have a priest. By "moving forward" he meant he was going to attempt, yet again, to have everyone's wages and Centrelink benefits to go into one bank account. His. Then he would personally dole out the money he believed everyone needed to live on and the rest would be for community welfare.

I knew that any excess would line his own pockets.

In addition to this everyone would be wearing those dreadful, ugly habits. For the umpteenth time I resisted, saying very little to Tony as he knew exactly how I felt about both of these subjects. I hated being called to meetings of any sort with Kamm, Broussard or Jan Williams. Not only didn't I trust them, they and their actions were despicable in my eyes. Once in the office, I quietly listened to both Kamm and Tony talk about the supposed progress of the community. Kamm congratulated Tony on going through with the subdiaconate orders. After which he turned to me saying in sickly sweet voice, "I heard you had a difficult time accepting this. If you'd like private counselling, I can give that to you." My sweet smile and polite refusal belied my true thoughts, which were: "You bastard. If either of your hands go anywhere within two feet of me, I'll cut your fingers off with a blunt knife."

When the meeting was over, I was relieved to be out of there.

Meanwhile I was still calling Scottie on a regular basis, telling him everything that was going on in the community and personally. He was horrified and disgusted by what was going on in the community. He saw it for the cult that is was. I just wanted to be heard by someone I trusted. I honestly thought he had my best interests at heart but he was using our friendship and my trust to gradually steer me back to the "True Faith," only I didn't realise it straight away.

Chapter 22 – Tuesday / Moving Day

As soon as I woke I was eager to begin the day. We still had more packing to do, but I wanted to get the lease signed as soon as possible, so we could start moving in.

I was impatient and had a hard time waiting till the afternoon. The hours seemed to drag, but soon enough it was time to go sign the papers at the Housing Commission before heading on to the real estate agent.

This was a momentous occasion because it was the first time I'd ever signed my name on a lease. The act of signing my name and not relying on anyone else made me feel like I had a little bit more control of my life. I was so proud that I'd done all of this myself -- without an ounce of help from Tony.

Many times, over the years he'd told me I was useless at making decisions or that it wasn't a woman's place to make important decisions, especially when it involved moving house. This act of signing a lease -- *my lease*--proved that everything Tony had said about me was flat out wrong, and it felt good to acknowledge that.

After I visited the real estate agent, I stood staring at the keys in my hand. I couldn't believe I actually had the key to a new house--and a new life. This was the first time ever, that I'd lived in a completely new house. What's more, it was a house I actually liked! I was disappointed that we couldn't begin moving things in that day, but it was too late in the afternoon to begin, so I went home. The older kids could barely contain their excitement about the move and the fact that they'd have the next day off to help move and set up the new house.

After dinner, I turned in early and slept soundly knowing that the next day would mark another of my moves toward freedom.

Chapter 23 – The Beginning of the End

After years of living in the cult, my marriage, which had been on shaky ground to begin with, was getting worse. Tony acted like a boarder in the house, doing his own thing, barely talking to me yet taking full advantage of me managing the house, the meals and the children. I didn't want to have sex with him anymore, but he insisted and I felt utterly sick and taken advantage of every time he had sex with me.

Finally, I couldn't take it anymore. One night when he came groping in the dark, I told him, "If you want sex with me, you can pay for it. Literally pay me like you would a prostitute." His hand retreated faster than you could say Jack Robinson and he never came near me again. After that I began to feel like I had a bit more control over my life, albeit in small ways. I had already mentally detached myself from the cult, and whenever I had to venture over that side of the property, I was friendly towards everyone, but never revealed what I was up to.

Tony had been gambling on and off since the beginning of our marriage, but in the past few years it had got much worse. I had confronted him many times about this awful habit, and each time he would get angry, ignore me or just walk out of the house. He often left his mail lying around, so I would see the credit card bills and the massive amounts he bet each time. It horrified me that he justified placing AU $1000 bets, several times a day yet, according to him, we couldn't afford new clothes or shoes for the children. Each week he would give me AU $250 to buy groceries for the ten of us, and every week I experienced a panic attack at the supermarket checkout. I always wrote a list and whittled it down before I left home, but each week I could feel my anxiety rise as the girl rung up my items and I had to decide what to keep and what to give back. It was so stressful and I decided it was time to take matters into my own hands.

My last baby, Kim, was only a few weeks old when I decided the time was right to go on a search. Even though I knew Tony would be away for a few days, I waited for about an hour after he left to ensure it was safe for me to search in peace. Elisa was posted as a lookout just in case Tony returned unexpectedly while I went into our bedroom cupboard where I'd seen Tony place the wads of cash that he had withdrawn from the bank.

He'd always had a mistrust of banks and regularly withdrew everything from his account. I wasn't entirely sure where he hid it, but systematically searched every pocket I could find. At first I only found a few hundred dollars here and there.

There must be more in here somewhere, I thought.

I searched again and found a hidden pocket in one of his suits that he barely wore anymore. I could feel a huge wad of notes and I dragged them all out and meticulously searched again to see if I'd missed anything. After failing to find any more money, I sat down on the floor to count the notes. I'd never seen so much money in my life! After counting it twice the amount came to AU $20,000. I was gobsmacked. I was having panic attacks at the supermarket checkout each week because I never had enough money to cover all the groceries and I was grinding wheat and other grains to bake bread from scratch, always scrounging around for food and clothes and he was not only hiding money from me but gambling it away by the thousands.

I realised that I needed to hide this money somewhere where Tony couldn't get it. Since I didn't have a bank account to deposit it into, I wondered what to do and came up with the idea to bury it. Our property was next to National Parks and Wildlife land, and no one was allowed on it. I grabbed a biscuit tin from the kitchen and stuffed all the notes inside and taped it closed tightly. Whilst my two youngest children were napping, I marched out to the shed where I took a shovel and walked into the bush. I found a fallen log and dug a deep hole underneath it, placed the tin inside and shoveled the dirt back on top. He wouldn't find it now!

By the time Tony arrived back home later that week, I'd forgotten all about what I'd done. I was changing my baby's nappy when he came into the lounge room. "Where's the money?" he angrily demanded.

"What money?" I asked before remembered what he was talking about. I'd gone too far now to turn back so I faced him. "Oh! That money. Well it's gone now. No one can touch it."

"What do you mean, no one can touch it? You took it so obviously you know where it is!" he shouted.

I kept insisting that no one could touch it and he was furious that I'd taken it and now refused to tell him where it was. This was the first time in my life I'd actually stood my ground with him and I was relieved to watch him leave the house.

After standing up to Tony the first time, I felt stronger and began looking for ways to make it possible to move. I had since transferred the AU $20K to a friend's bank account where it was held in trust, so even I had no access to it, which meant I still didn't have any money at my immediate disposal. However, I kept a positive attitude and began looking at the real estate section of the newspaper Tony bought home each week. He noticed that I was spending some time having a look and asked what I was doing. I was just brushed off his questions. The next week I noticed he threw some newspaper into the bin as he walked inside. After he finished reading the paper, I went to take a look at the real estate section. It wasn't there. I very casually asked where the real estate section was. "Oh, they're not printing that section anymore." "Ahuh", I thought to myself. When he went out later I searched the bin. Sure enough I found the real estate section. I confronted him when he came home, he wasn't happy that I'd found it and caught him in a lie. The next week he binned that section whilst still in town so there was no evidence when he came home. I was angry because I now understood that he was trying to control me and keep me from moving out. I knew I'd find a way to move my kids and I out, no matter how many roadblocks he put in my way.

I'd heard through the grapevine that there were unhappy members who had decided to move out. Kamm's ongoing trial was revealing more dirty details, details that quite simply could not be denied or explained away anymore. The hard evidence was there for all to see. I myself had been able to read the letters that Kamm had written to one victim. I wished I was able to move like some of these other people were. It made me feel a bit low but I knew if I was patient my time would come.

As I was doing a "clean sweep" of completely cutting myself off from the cult, I wanted the children to attend school elsewhere. I'd attempted to home-school my eldest two for a little bit, but my heart wasn't in it because I had bad memories of own home-schooling experience. Besides I wanted them to enjoy their school years, have a big circle of friends and experiences that I never had. We found a Christian school on the other side of Nowra and made enquiries. There was an extensive interview process which of course included knowing where we lived, it wasn't difficult to know that just looking at me. The changes in my life had not yet included my dress which was still very conservative and out of place, but I wasn't going to be deterred by anything that would stop my kids from having a better life.

Tony as usual tried to skirt around the issue about us still living in the cult but I was very upfront about us moving as soon as we could. At first the Christian school only had enough room for the two eldest children, but assured us the rest would follow suit soon after. The older children were so relieved to be out of the cult school, it made me very happy to have them amongst normal people. The staff, pupils and families that made up Nowra Christian School were very welcoming, understanding and helpful. Everyone made my children's transition to school life very smooth and I was so grateful for that. The kids were now catching the bus to and from school, life was beginning to look more normal.

Tony was spending more and more time away working in Goulburn, which made my life and the kids' lives much happier and easier. I relaxed our strict routine and we attempted to live as normal lives as possible, although I was still very Catholic in my thinking and dress. We all knew the unspoken rule when Tony came back, that we had to behave as he liked to make it easier.

One occasion when Tony was home I had to go out on a day when it was pouring rain. Although my trust in Tony minding the children was low, I asked him to babysit them whilst I was away for two hours. I prepared their food and drink and even folded nappies, in case he needed to change them. I literally ran around town to get done in the shortest time possible and arrived home right on the two-hour mark.

As I drove up the driveway I could see that Tony was still at the computer. I felt anger rise up inside me, I knew he hadn't moved the whole time I was gone. I opened up the car door and, even before I entered the house, I heard the children crying.

Angry and really worried, I flew into the house to find both little children standing in the kitchen, crying their hearts out. Tony had hurriedly shut down the computer when he saw me coming and was standing in the kitchen looking useless. I ignored him, giving all my attention to my babies. One of them had a dirty nappy and broken glass was all over the floor. I hurriedly checked both of them for cuts and blood and found they were in one piece. I settled them both, changed their nappies, gave them a drink and then questioned Tony about what he did whilst I was gone. *I knew* he was lying but I gave him the chance to answer me honestly. He tried telling me that he had looked after them and they were fine till they began crying, for apparently no reason. "Ahuh," I thought, "children cry for no reason." I'd already surmised that Ellie had gotten thirsty and climbed the bench to reach for a glass, which had crashed to the floor. And he'd done nothing. "What would happen to the children if something happened to me, who would look after them?" I asked him tightly. "Oh, I'd pay someone to look after them," he told me. "No, you wouldn't, you're a scrooge. You'd just give them away," I angrily answered him. From that day on, I never allowed him to mind them again, I knew I could never trust him.

I was still confiding in Scottie on a regular basis and travelling down to Goulburn a few times a month. It felt good to safely confide in someone but some things he was saying weren't sitting well with me. My entire life had been one of indoctrination, manipulation and following strict rules on daily, even a minutely basis, with threats of punishments, reparation and hellfire. I'd never had the opportunity to question any of these beliefs that had been shoved down my throat and now I was just on the cusp of exploration. Scottie knew my marriage was over yet he still told me on every available occasion that I was married for life. Tony and I didn't necessarily have to live together but we had to stay faithful to one another. I was to keep wearing my wedding ring till one of us died and under no circumstances was I to be ever alone with a man or amongst a group of men. "Look what Eve did to Adam, she tempted him and he sinned." Once again, it was all about the woman being the temptress, man not being able to control his urges. He also attempted to use humour in telling me I was old and unattractive. Whenever he mentioned it I laughed it off and jokingly argued with him but he was able to quickly wind me down because he had a better understanding of the church's teaching. I didn't yet have enough life experience in order to be able to stand my ground and debate him.

Something else that I knew I needed to do was open a bank account. I'd not stepped foot into a bank for years, I had no idea what was needed to open a bank account nor which bank to choose. I decided to open an account with the same bank Tony used because I thought it would be easier. But I was petrified of them telling Tony that I now had my own account. I was a bundle of nerves as I walked into the bank and needed help in filling out the forms because I didn't know what to do. I sighed with relief on the way out but it was short lived because now I needed to go tell the welfare agency.

I hated going into our local welfare agency, Nowra was a low socio-economic area and I felt uncomfortable amongst all the rough people. The other thing that made me nervous were all the forms to fill out. Tony had always filled out the welfare paperwork and just told me where to sign. I grit my teeth, lined up and put out a little prayer that I would get a helpful understanding person. I was so lucky! A lovely lady helped me understand and fill out the paperwork and I changed my bank details too.

I still had to face Tony to tell him what I'd done. I knew he wouldn't like it and try to make trouble, so I decided to stretch the truth. In order to get it over and done with I told him almost as soon as he came home. "Welfare called me to say that there's a new ruling whereby the payments have to go into the mother's account, so I was forced to open my own account." Phew. It was done. He met my announcement with silence. I think he was beginning to realise that the horse had bolted so to speak, there was no stopping his willful wife.

#

By now I was regularly attending mass at local parishes. Nowra was a big area that contained a number of churches, so I began to explore which church I liked best. I'd found out that Fr. Ronan, in Kangaroo Valley, was a monk who held onto more of the old Catholic ways, so I decided to go check him out. His parish was just a little church, but beautifully kept. There were gorgeous gardens outside, but when you stepped inside the church you were transported back in time! The familiar fragrance of incense brought back lovely childhood memories for me. As soon as I saw Fr. Ronan, I felt peace come over me.

He had a quiet commanding presence, very kind, understanding and helpful. He welcomed me back into the fold of the church without judgement.

One of Fr. Ronan's faithful parishioners was Cynthia.

The first time we attended mass there, she made a point of introducing herself. She was a very motherly lady, a former nurse who was quite knowledgeable about mental health. When we got to know her better, she told me that she could see Tony had mental health issues as soon as she saw him. She sized me up pretty quickly too, in fact she understood me better than I understood myself. She came to visit us whilst we were still living in the cult and often called me to see how I was. She loved the children and had them stay over at her house which was lovely because my children's grandparents lived in another state. It was she who kindly took me aside and suggested I have help when colouring my hair, as I'd missed a bit and it was noticeable. It was the first time in my life that I'd coloured my hair and I appreciated that she cared enough to tell me. Cynthia was the one who first encouraged me to make time for me, she stressed the importance of making time to be alone, relax. Although I agreed with her, I didn't know how to go about it. I'd never had time by myself, I didn't really know what it meant.

As I refused to attend mass in the cult anymore, sometimes Tony would come with me. He'd always had the habit of doing his own thing when attending parish services and often it was opposite to what was going on around him. I was embarrassed to have him act like this just when I was doing my best to be normal and fit in. The mass service wasn't like I'd been used to growing up either, but I figured life goes on and changes must be made. I was tired of always having to stand up for everything. Besides, after having been ordained by Broussard, Tony had excommunicated himself from the mainstream Catholic church and I didn't want his excommunication standing in my way of moving forward with a new life. I didn't know how to verbalise it then, but I felt like he was a rock hanging round my neck, weighing me down.

It was one of these Sunday's at Kangaroo Valley that we first met the Bishop of Wollongong, Bishop Peter Ingham. For many years he had tried to reason with Kamm, but the latter was always very pig-headed and refused to listen or obey his local bishop. Quite literally, Kamm was a thorn in Bishop Peter's side. Kamm had never painted a nice picture of Bishop Peter and in many of his "messages" there were supposed to be punishments raining down on the Bishop for disobeying Our Lady. Having recently experienced such a warm welcome from the local parishes, I was curious to meet Bishop Peter to see for myself what kind of person he was.

I was not disappointed. He was a lovely, warm, understanding gentleman, and was keen to hear my story as it was difficult for him to gain a proper picture of who was living in the community, how strong their beliefs were and how many followers Kamm actually had. Bishop Peter was eager to help make people feel welcome coming back into the fold of the church. When Tony first met

Bishop Peter, Tony led him to believe that he was defending the bishop to Kamm and Broussard. In reality, Tony was trying to justify the priestly orders he had received and *still* be a part of the mainstream church. A foot in each camp so to speak.

Bishop Peter moved swiftly to put things in place in order to support the members leaving the cult in sorting out their standing in the church. Although we weren't yet moving, we also received these papers.

Cynthia knew the bishop quite well also some of his office staff, so she spoke to them on my and behalf. She was able to articulate things that I didn't even know and hadn't come to understand yet. There was a query of the validity of our marriage in the Catholic Church because when we got married in 1988, the priests of the Society of St. Pius X had been excommunicated, thus making our vows invalid. For me, it felt kind of weird to be in this limbo. Any couple from the cult who had been married by Broussard was given the choice to retake their vows or just get divorced since, in quite a few cases, the marriages had been pre-arranged. That was not how it happened with Tony and I, so initially I thought to do the correct thing and just get married again, in a private ceremony. Part of me felt uneasy about this because when I thought of spending the rest of my life with Tony it made me die inside.

On the other hand, I couldn't imagine myself as a single mother, and deep down I believed my children deserved a father, and an irresponsible, uncaring one was better than none. Having been completely indoctrinated in the Catholic faith, I just couldn't think past that. Until one day I received a phone call from Sr. Moya, the Canon Lawyer. She explained to me that I was under no obligation to remarry Tony, I needed to make the best decision for *me*, not anyone else. Not to be guilted into it. "But my children deserve a father," I told her. "What about *you*? You also deserve a life of happiness," she replied. Well. That certainly was something to think about. That choice had never been expressed to me before. Suddenly I actually had the choice *not* to be married to Tony for the rest of my life and what's more, I was being given permission to do so by a Canon Lawyer.

I was recounting this conversation to Cynthia a few days later when she told me that she'd had honest words with Sr. Moya, telling her that it was clear Tony had mental health issues, he wasn't treating the children and I very well, I was basically a single mother anyway because he never helped me and to top it all off, he was a serious gambler. Cynthia went on to tell me that Sr. Moya had already spoken to Bishop Peter who was going to send out a letter to both of us with instructions to have pre- marriage counseling before any vows could be renewed.

Cynthia, Sr. Moya and I all knew that Tony wouldn't have a bar of it, he hated being told what to do and there'd be no way he'd go for counseling. He was being given a spiritual direction to follow, if he didn't, then the marriage was over. We were correct! When the letter arrived a few days later and Tony read it he said there was no need for pre-marriage counseling because we'd already been married for seventeen years. I had no idea how to go about getting a divorce, I actually had so much to deal with right at that moment, I decided to put it aside for now.

Bishop Peter had also organised for free counseling for those members who were leaving or who were considering leaving the cult. I'd never been to counseling and had no idea what to expect but instinctively knew I'd be needing some sort of help. So, I secretly made an appointment and went along. I outlined my story, living in the cult, my feelings about that, the lack of money, Tony not treating the children or me well, his depression, the list went on. The hour passed very quickly. After I'd revealed all that, the male counsellor said to me, "Well we really need to get your husband in here to hear his side of the story." My heart sank. Tony would be so angry to know I'd revealed "secrets" because he always maintained that what went on behind closed doors, stayed behind those doors. Assuming he knew what he was talking about I made another appointment for the next week, somehow I needed to figure out how to get Tony to attend.

I made up some vague story about needing him to come with me to talk to someone, so he reluctantly came with me. The counsellor opened with my "lack of money" comment. Tony looked annoyed then said, "If she wants more money, then all she has to do is ask for it and I'll give it to her. I don't see what the problem is. Everything else is fine." I was shocked. I'd known him not to tell the full truth before, but to tell a bare faced lie was beyond the pale. My faith in counsellors was lost that day, I couldn't believe that I'd actually reached out for help, only to have the counsellor believe my husband over me. Once again, Tony was angry that I'd gone to an outsider for help and had deceived him into going.

As time went on I felt more and more separate from Tony and Sr. Moya's words kept playing in the back of my mind. I definitely didn't want to stay married to him and he wasn't making one ounce of effort to treat me as his wife. I'd put in seventeen years of hard yards, I was over it. All of those years I'd faithfully wore my wedding ring but lately I had begun to feel the weight of it on my finger. One day I decided to take it off and never looked back. The next time I saw Scottie he noticed I'd taken it off and wasn't happy. He vainly tried to convince me to put it back on but I wasn't turning back. I was out to live my own life, not to follow rules anymore.

I began to research Canon Law, The Catechism of the Catholic Church and Pastoral Theology. I'm by no means an expert, but since Tony had these books lying around I decided to put them to good use. My research told me exactly what I'd always known, quite simply, it came down to two clear rules.

The Eastern and Western Rites were never meant to be co joined and there had never been married priests in the Western Rite.

Besides, it all had to defined by the Catholic Church, no mere man could change it. I began to write letters to Broussard, only one-page letters, asking for "enlightenment" regarding those two rules. I wanted Broussard and Kamm to see that despite trying to pull the wool over our eyes, it was plainly stated in the rules of the Catholic Church that what was happening in the cult, was wrong. Tony suggested that I write it only from myself and that I not include him reasoning that if it came only from me then we couldn't be kicked out of our house because of something I was doing on my own. He knew I was right, but he also knew he couldn't control me and wouldn't support me.

Broussard was surprised to receive this letter, his response was almost a thesis, based only on Our Lady's messages to her favourite son, "The Little Pebble" aka Kamm. He was also a bit put out I'd dared to question anything, let alone his authority. As his response was completely inadequate and not based on Catholicism, I patiently wrote a second another letter asking the same questions in a different way. His response was a bit longer still and he was annoyed that I'd written a second time. He also wrote that he'd heard I was attending mass in the parish, did that mean my belief in Kamm was shaky? His response contained nothing but his usual waffle, he still hadn't made the connection that I'd figured out what he and Kamm were doing was totally against the Catholic Church, to whom they claimed to be faithful. I decided to give Broussard one last chance and repeated my questions in a third letter. He was affronted that I was like a dog with a bone, he'd *never* had to deal with someone as stubborn as this before. Although he'd shown my other letters to Kamm, even this one tipped Kamm over the edge. Kamm himself penned a response where I was told to stop questioning his authority or we would be asked to leave. I was actually hoping we would be. All my letters had been put before the community council, which Kamm had set up some time before in a weak attempt to squash dogged rumours that he made all the decisions. Everyone knew it was ridiculous because it didn't make an ounce of difference what was said or what decision was made in those meetings by the members as Kamm always overruled them. I knew two of those members quite well and they had been very outspoken at times against Kamm also. They could see my argument to a point but when my third letter arrived on the table they urged me to stop because I'd received adequate answers already. "You are right, but these are very different times, Our Lady's requests over rule the Laws of the Church. Please stop causing trouble." I smiled sweetly but knew in my heart I was right.

I continued to quietly dig my heels in and attended church in the local parish.

Word got back to me that my actions were "giving bad example" to the rest of the community. The members were instructed not to speak with me nor spend any time with me.

Being a friendly, outgoing girl Kamm and Broussard were afraid I would easily influence other members and they would wind up with a rebellion on their hands. I knew in my heart that what I was doing was right, and that it was time to take a stand. I discovered that whenever I saw other members, whether in the community or elsewhere they would avert their eyes and try to ignore me. It didn't worry me in the slightest. I still waved and greeted people which made them feel terribly uncomfortable because they were forced to answer.

I felt lighter as I walked around the compound. My resistance had given me hope that things would get better, and before long, they were.

Although I liked going to mass at Kangaroo Valley I found the Berry church a little bit closer, so it became our regular Sunday attendance. The congregation were just lovely, so welcoming, understanding, supportive. There was an elderly gentleman who played the organ beautifully too. I loved hearing organ music again. One Sunday when Tony was with us he made a comment to the organist that there were quite a few wrong notes. "Well I've been playing for many years now, there aren't any young ones who are interested to learn and I have arthritis," the gentleman replied. "My wife knows how to play," Tony helpfully suggested.

When I heard about this exchange later on I was shocked on two accounts, first that Tony could be so rude as to mention wrong notes, especially as he was no musician and second, that he pushed me forward.

I was standing outside in the sunshine when I saw this lovely gentleman come down the steps. He stretched out his hand, "I'm Geoff and I'm the organist. Your husband mentioned that you play. You're the woman I always wanted to meet! Would you like me to teach you how to play the organ?" Straight away I loved his sense of humour and just said "Yes, I'd love to," without thinking.

It was the beginning of a beautiful musical friendship. I had learnt the piano for over a decade when I was younger and although I'd played a keyboard for the cult services, this was different. I'd not played a two-manual organ before.

Geoff and I met at the church every Friday morning for months, he introduced me to beautiful music from composers I'd never heard of, taught me the finesse of playing smoothly and shared pearls of wisdom as we talked. We had a common love of Bach, "After mass send the congregation out with a bang," Geoff used to say, "nice and loud to start their week well!" He gave me music that he and his father had played back in England. He never judged me for wearing a big scarf over my head when I was in the church. Often the congregation asked him questions to pass onto me because they wanted to understand me and my journey better. The children and I felt so much warmth, love and acceptance from these beautiful parishioners.

After months of learning various pieces of music Geoff announced one Friday that I'd be playing for mass the next week. I thought he only meant one piece of music, so I was prepared for that. I'd always been nervous about playing in public but also loved making music. When I arrived at the church he told me I'd be playing the whole mass. It made me so nervous. But he stood by my side the whole hour, supporting me, turning pages, telling me when to start and stop. I fumbled a bit, there were a few wrong notes but I enjoyed it too.

It was my baptism by fire and the congregation loved me so much they gave me a standing ovation! I was proud to play for them, and the parishioners helped me by minding my children when I played. This was the type of community I'd been searching for, and when I played the organ for Sunday services, I felt like I'd found my home.

Chapter 24 – Wednesday / The Day After

It was finally moving day, and I woke early because I was so excited to get started. It was difficult to contain the kids because they were eager to just move, and to hell with everything else!

After a quick breakfast Elisa and I packed the last of the kitchen things. Tony had decided that we'd move everything via trailers instead of a truck, so when he was ready to go, Elisa went with him and stayed at the house to unpack things as they were unloaded.

Just as Tony was about to leave, I noticed Peter Jirgens had arrived along with another unknown gentleman. I'd seen his face around the school but never met Brett, the assistant pastor of the Nowra

Christian Church. On the previous Sunday, Margie had asked for extra hands to help us move and he'd shown up.

Tony seemed surprisingly cooperative and I was just going with it whilst it lasted. I couldn't wait to see the back of this property, the sooner the better. Despite having three trailers going back and forth all morning, it took longer than I'd anticipated to empty the house. All too soon, it was 10:45am and suddenly I saw that the Sheriff had arrived.

I walked over to greet him. He kindly asked how we were doing and whether we had taken everything out of the house yet. He told me he needed to change the locks and paste notices on the windows, so I walked with him to the house and told him not to bother changing the locks. "You have no idea how grateful I am for this opportunity to move. Here are all the keys, save yourself the time because I'll never be back." He then told me that as long as we had everything out of the house, we could take the rest of the day to move what we had left.

Finally, the car was full of the last household things that I'd wanted, and I drove to our new house. Elisa had done such a wonderful job of arranging the kitchen and organizing the furniture into the various rooms that the house looked very neat already! I just knew the kids and I would be happy here.

Margie was unpacking some kitchen things when I arrived and she asked me if I minded her arranging my pantry. "Of course not. I'd love that, thank you!" I replied. I was so caught up in getting beds made for that night that I didn't realise Margie had disappeared for a while. I came back downstairs to see Margie carrying boxes of groceries inside and placing them in my new pantry. She had gone out shopping for pantry staples and proceeded to fill the cupboard with the new food. My heart felt so full from the generosity of this lovely lady. I'd not experienced this "practice what you preach" before since the Catholics I'd known had all preached but not actually practiced these simple virtues. It suddenly hit me that I'd not felt this loved and cared for, in a very long time.

Unfortunately, Tony was moving with us, but Scottie had him working almost full time down in Goulburn, so he wouldn't be around as the kids and I adjusted to our new lives.

Later that day, when all of my kids were home from school, they could barely contain their excitement! It was the first time we'd lived in a two-story house and they absolutely loved it. I especially loved my new bedroom, it was large, light and airy with an en-suite bathroom and, much like the beginning of my new life, it was all my own now.

www.ingramcontent.com/pod-product-compliance
Lightning Source LLC
Chambersburg PA
CBHW051937290426
44110CB00015B/2009